OUR MISSION

We publish books that empower people's lives.

RODALE BOOKS

CREATIVE IDEAS FOR COLOR AND FABRIC EDITORIAL AND DESIGN STAFF

Editor: *Karen Costello Soltys*
Designer: *Tanya L. Lipinski*
Photographer: *Mitch Mandel*
Illustrators: *Mario Ferro and Jackie Walsh*
Photo Stylist: *Marianne Grape Laubach*
Copy Editor: *Erana Bumbardatore*
Manufacturing Coordinator: *Patrick Smith*

Distributed in the book trade by St. Martin's Press

2 4 6 8 10 9 7 5 3   hardcover

RODALE HOME AND GARDEN BOOKS

Vice President and Editorial Director:
Margaret Lydic Balitas
Managing Editor, Quilt Books: *Suzanne Nelson*
Art Director: *Michael Mandarano*
Associate Art Director: *Mary Ellen Fanelli*
Studio Manager: *Leslie Keefe*
Copy Director: *Dolores Plikaitis*
Office Manager: *Karen Earl-Braymer*

If you have any questions or comments concerning the editorial content of this book, please write to:
Rodale Press, Inc.
Book Readers' Service
33 East Minor Street
Emmaus, PA 18098

The photo of Amish Easter Baskets on page 44 appears courtesy of the Collection of the Museum of the American Quilter's Society, Paducah, Ky. Photo by DSI Studios, Evansville, Ind.

Library of Congress Cataloging-in-Publication Data

McKelvey, Susan Richardson.
The classic American quilt collection. Creative ideas for color and fabric / Susan McKelvey.
    p. cm.
    Includes bibliographical references and index.
    ISBN 0–87596–726–4 (alk. paper) (hc)
    1. Quilts. 2. Color in textile crafts. 3. Patchwork.
I. Title.
TT835.M4497   1996
746.46—dc20   96–1127

THE CLASSIC AMERICAN
QUILT COLLECTION®

Creative Ideas for
COLOR and FABRIC

Susan McKelvey

 Rodale Press, Emmaus, Pennsylvania

Contents

Introduction

Color is not the mystery it seems to be. It follows rules, conforms to principles, and is, therefore, predictable. In this book I've taken color theory and translated it into terms that are easy for quilters to understand and use. You can plan the look of any quilt once you know a few simple color principles. No more hit or miss quilts! Suppose you want to make a quilt that soothes viewers and wraps them in a peaceful feeling. Knowing a few simple color rules will help you achieve that. Do you want to create a quilt with a happy, buoyant feeling? You can do it. A restful, calm quilt? Whatever your goal, once you're familiar with the concepts covered in this book, it's totally within your grasp.

Once you understand how color works, you can emphasize any part of a design you choose—perhaps a flower, a bird, a basket, the sashing, or the border. By incorporating what you know about how color works into the plans for your quilts, you can be certain that one part of a quilt will not overwhelm another. You'll be able to add exciting accents to exactly the right spots in any project. The possibilities are endless.

You'll also be able to look at parts of quilts and analyze why they work (or why they don't). For example, take a look at the two pairs of quilt blocks shown on this page. After working through this book, you'll be able to figure out why one flower stands out against the white background more than the other in the **Flower Basket Blocks** illustration. You'll also know why the two **Joseph's Coat Blocks** look so different even though they are made using the same set of colors.

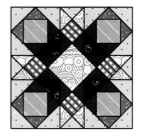

Joseph's Coat Blocks

Being able to look at quilts this way doesn't take years of art training—it just takes knowing the right kinds of questions to ask. Once you've asked the right questions and found the answers, you're well on your way to understanding how different colors behave. Once you can do that, it's easy to make color work the way you want it to in your quilts.

Intrigued? Nothing is more fun to play with than color. Nothing gives you such a feeling of confidence in quiltmaking as being able to plan more successful quilts because you know what the colors you have chosen will do.

Come join me in an exploration of color and fabric. I've used color photographs of many quilts from other books in *The Classic American Quilt Collection* as examples, as they may be familiar to you. I've also included both antique and new quilts because color theory applies to all quilts and all fabrics within them. By learning just a little about color, you'll see that any quilt pattern, traditional or not, can be changed in countless ways, and you'll be empowered to make color and fabric decisions with confidence. So get ready for an uncomplicated introduction to color theory and fabric styles, and feel the excitement of color sweep into your life and into your quilts.

Susan McKelvey

Susan McKelvey

Flower Basket Blocks

USING THIS BOOK

This book is designed as a workbook, a tool for you to use as you learn about the different aspects of color. As we discuss the color terms on the following pages, many of which may be new to you, take time out to make your own examples of the terms. There is no better way to learn about a concept and truly understand how it works than to experiment with it. You probably have fabrics in your scrap basket that you've sewn with, but you may not have thought about them in terms of color. I encourage you to use your own fabrics to learn the color concepts in this book, since these fabrics will be the foundations or accents for many of your future quilts.

Pasting up fabric swatches is a wonderful and quick way to practice the principles of color. We've provided plenty of color exercises and space for you to incorporate your fabrics into this workbook. Use rubber cement or a glue stick so the pages don't warp and pucker. If you prefer not to paste directly into your book, make photocopies of the color exercise pages and paste your samples on them. Keep your copied pages in a notebook labeled Color and Fabric so you can refer back to the appropriate pages as necessary to review a particular topic. Wherever you decide to paste your fabrics, just remember that it's important that you do make the fabric samples. When you look back later, your fabrics will be far better reminders than the samples I have provided, because you chose and thought about them. So try to make your pasteups different from the ones I've provided. That way, they'll be of more help to you later.

If you want your swatches to be perfect shapes, make a paper template to guide you in cutting the swatches. Some people want their samples to be perfect; to others that's not so important. Follow your own preferences, and don't worry if you don't have enough examples of a particular concept to fill the space provided. Paste up what you have, or consider working with friends. You will have far more fabrics to choose from if you get a group of quilters together to share, and your friends will enjoy learning about color and fabrics just as much as you will.

Last, do the color exercises as you go. It's easier to learn about color if you read an idea, understand it, and then follow up by working with your own fabrics in relation to that idea. When you've mastered one concept, then you're ready to move on to the next.

So get out your fabric, scissors, and glue stick, and get ready to have fun learning about color and fabrics!

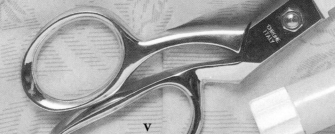

THE COLOR WHEEL

THE COLOR WHEEL

You don't have to be an artist to use basic color principles in your quiltmaking. The color wheel is a wonderful tool—it provides a colorful, visual way to learn and share a common color vocabulary. Some of the terminology that follows may be familiar to you, some may be new. But learning the lingo is the best way to be sure we are all talking about the same thing when we discuss and study color.

In this book we will study a 12-color wheel, with each color on the wheel distinct from all others. It is by varying these colors—making them darker, lighter, or combining two of them—that all other colors are formed. Once you learn a few basic principles of color, you will become more confident in selecting colors and mixing fabrics in your quilting projects.

COLOR WHEEL VOCABULARY

PURE COLORS

The 12 colors on the **The Color Wheel** are rich, vivid colors, as shown below. They are, for example, the reddest red and the greenest green possible. Quite simply, they are all the most intense versions of themselves. Therefore, they are called *pure* or *intense* colors.

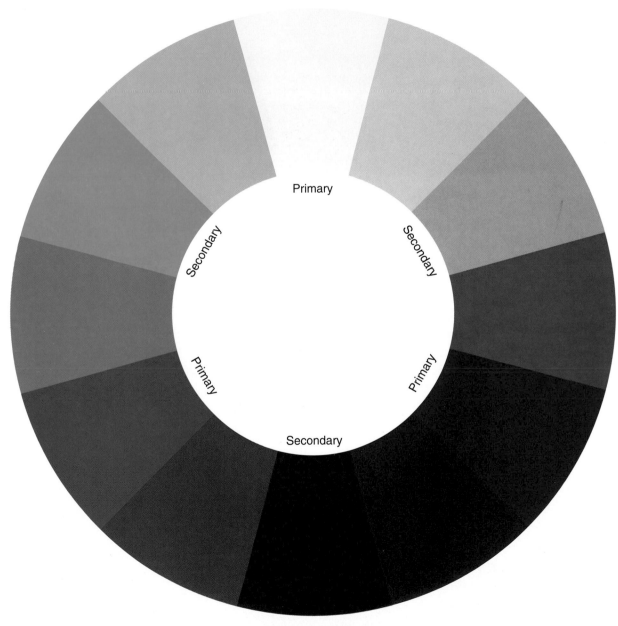

The Color Wheel

PRIMARY AND SECONDARY COLORS

The primary colors—which you probably remember from elementary school art classes—are red, blue, and yellow. They are set on the color wheel at points that are equal distances from each other, thus forming an equilateral triangle, as shown in red in **Primary and Secondary Colors** at right. All pure colors are derived from them.

If we were painters, we could mix the three primary colors together to make all of the other colors on the wheel, including the secondary colors, which are green

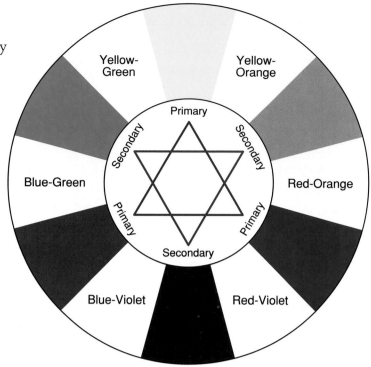

Primary and Secondary Colors

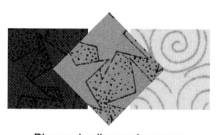

Blue and yellow make green

Red and yellow make orange

Red and blue make violet

(equal parts of blue and yellow), orange (equal parts of red and yellow), and violet (equal parts of red and blue), as shown at left. Notice that the secondary colors are halfway between the primary colors and also form an equilateral triangle, shown in blue on the color wheel above. These pure colors—red, blue, yellow, orange, purple, and green—are the most powerful colors because they cause the greatest visual impact. The other six colors are formed by mixing the primary and secondary colors.

VALUE

Any color on the color wheel can be made lighter or darker, and that process is called varying the color's *value*. Values of a color that are darker than the pure color on the color wheel are called *shades*, while values that are lighter than the pure color are called *tints*.

Continuing with our painting analogy, an artist simply needs to add black paint to a pure color to make a shade of that pure color. The greater the percentage of black added, the darker the shade of the original color. For instance, if black is added to pure blue, you'll end up with a shade such as navy blue, as shown at the top of the **Blue Color Values** chart. On the other hand, by adding white to pure blue, you'll achieve a tint such as baby blue or powder blue, as shown at the bottom of the chart.

If you hear quilters talking about how many shades of a color they used in their quilts, they're probably using the word shade to refer to how many different color *values* they used. Quilters rarely use the terms shade and tint, so to be clear we'll simply refer to light, medium, and dark values.

Make a Value Sample

Referring to the **Blue Color Values** chart for guidance and following the directions on page 6, use your own fabrics to make a sample set of values in one color. While mixing paints to create different color values is an easy process, selecting fabrics of different color values can be a bit trickier. After all, unless you are dying your own fabrics, your color palette is limited to the fabrics in your sewing room. Don't be discouraged if this exercise seems a bit tricky at first; the benefit of trying this technique is that you'll soon be looking at color in a whole new way! And you can always fill in the gaps in your value sample during your next visit to a quilt shop.

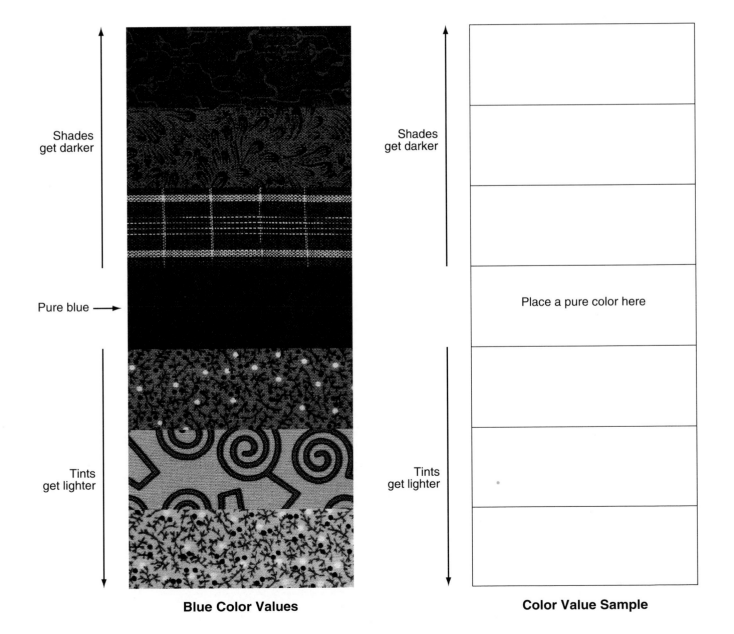

Blue Color Values   **Color Value Sample**

Make your first value sample using your favorite color. You're bound to have many fabric choices in this color, so you should have a greater variety of values on hand, and your selection process will be easier.

Step 1. Pull out all the fabrics you have in the color you've chosen and spread them out in front of you. Organize them from dark to light.

If you find it difficult to tell which of two fabrics is lighter or darker, view them from across the room. This will make subtle distinctions between values easier to detect.

Step 2. Using the **Color Value Sample** chart on page 5, paste the *purest* color in the center rec-

tangle of the chart. Then lay out the other fabrics by value. Paste up tints below the pure color and shades above the pure color, just as in the blue color values example.

INTENSITY

The 12 colors on the wheel can be varied in a second way, by changing their *intensity*. Remember, the colors on the wheel are described as being the most intense or purest versions of themselves. When gray is added to colors they become toned down, or duller and weaker in intensity. Therefore, a *tone* is simply a grayed version of a pure color.

Clear, bright versions of colors in several values

Grayed versions (tones) of same colors

Color Intensity

The grayness of colors is one of the hardest concepts to see, although we use it all the time. When faced with a large stack of fabrics, it is sometimes hard to see the slight differences in color intensity. Study the fabric examples in the **Color Intensity** chart on the opposite page to see how different a grayed version of a color can look from the pure color.

Make an Intensity Sample

Step 1. From your fabric stash, pull out colors for which you have many different intensities. Find as many examples of different intensities as you can. You might be surprised to find that your collection probably contains many low-intensity fabrics.

Step 2. As with the color value example, lay your fabrics on the table in front of you and separate them into groups by color.

Step 3. Within each color group, locate the purest color. Paste a swatch of each to the left column of the **Color Intensity Sample** chart below. Then find grayed or toned-down swatches of each color and paste them in the right column.

When making your samples, avoid crinkles in your paper by using a glue stick or brush-on rubber cement to paste your fabric samples. These work well even on photocopy paper, so don't be afraid to use either type of glue if you're pasting samples on copies of your book pages.

Paste clear colors here   Paste grayed versions here

Color Intensity Sample

More Color Terms and Color Schemes

Once you are familiar with the basic terms used to refer to the color wheel, you can use them to plan and discuss quilts and color schemes. But first, there are a few more color terms and concepts that are important to know.

Neutrals

A *neutral* is actually a noncolor. Black, white, and gray are *true neutrals,* as they contain no color. Neutrals are useful in any quilt, since they act as resting places for the eyes. They also soften colors that are placed next to them, and they make good backgrounds. As you'll see, neutrals contribute to many of the color schemes discussed later.

Quilters regularly use muslin and light beiges as neutrals, so they can be considered *quilters' neutrals.* Technically, of course, they are not neutral since they do contain some color. But because these light beiges are so close to being colorless, quilters use them all the time for backgrounds, where they act as neutrals. See **Neutrals,** below.

 *The secret to keeping beiges neutral is to use light or medium values. Dark beige becomes brown, which is a very strong, dark color, not a neutral.*

True Neutrals

Quilters' Neutrals

Neutrals

Make a Neutrals Sample

Go through your fabrics and pick out some prints, not solids, that are neutral. You're bound to have many, as most quilters incorporate neutrals into every quilt. Choose some true neutrals (black, gray, and white), as well as some quilters' neutrals (light beiges and off-whites).

Paste your fabric neutrals on the **Neutrals Sample** chart below to keep a record of all types of neutrals quilters use.

Paste up true neutrals

Paste up quilters' neutrals

Neutrals Sample

MONOCHROMATIC OR ONE-COLOR SCHEMES

Mono means one, and *chromo* means color. Together, monochromatic simply means a one-color scheme, and it's the easiest color scheme to work with. To plan a quilt with a one-color scheme, first choose only one of the 12 colors from the color wheel. If you wish, you may add any neutral background fabric, or you may simply stick to assorted values of your one color.

Monochromatic color schemes are easy to work with because there are not a lot of choices to be made. At the same time, because there isn't much variety, a monochromatic quilt can become boring if you're not careful.

If you decide to limit yourself to one color, include fabrics in many values, intensities, or tones to add variety and interest to your overall quilt design.

Monochromatic Example

The section of the **Courthouse Steps** quilt shown below is an excellent example of a monochromatic quilt. This quilt primarily uses shades of browns and quilters' neutrals, which are themselves very light shades of brown. The quiltmaker added lots of variety in the value of the brown fabrics and even more variety in the prints she selected, but it remains a one-color quilt.

As you can see, although the color scheme was limited to just one color (except for a stray purple, green, or blue print) and the quilt block itself is quite simple, the graphic impact is very dramatic in this antique quilt.

Courthouse Steps
by Ann Fryer, owned by Randolph County Historical Society, Moberly, Missouri

ANALOGOUS COLOR SCHEMES

Colors that are right next to each other on the color wheel are called *analogous* colors. The beauty of analogous colors is that they *always* coordinate or go together. Knowing about analogous colors provides every quiltmaker with a variety of useful color schemes, each guaranteed to be successful.

The reason analogous colors go together so well is that they are very similar. Choose two, three, or even four analogous colors to create your color scheme, and you will automatically have a pleasing color combination. Just take a look at the **Analogous Colors** fabric swatches on the opposite page. See how easily the colors blend together?

You can begin an analogous color scheme at any point on the color wheel. Whether you choose red, yellow, or purple as your starting point, the color you begin with plus its surrounding colors will match beautifully.

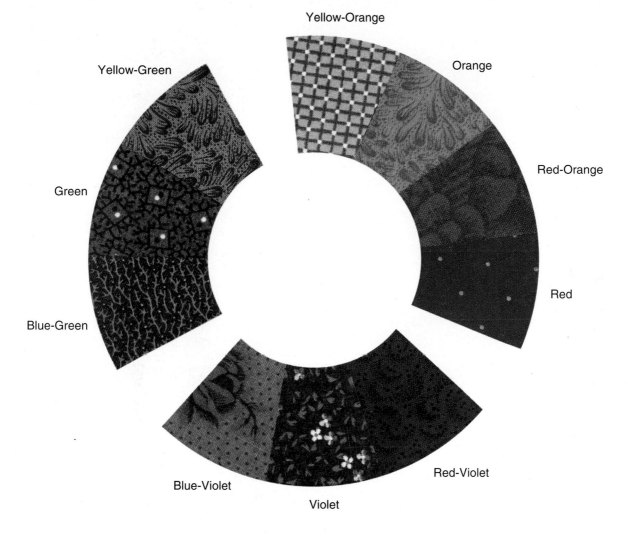

Yellow-Orange

Orange

Yellow-Green

Red-Orange

Green

Red

Blue-Green

Red-Violet

Blue-Violet

Violet

Analogous Colors

Make Analogous Color Schemes

Using the color wheel as your guide, select several sets of analogous colors and paste up your examples in the **Analogous Colors Sample** chart, shown below. You can expand the variety of fabrics by choosing fabrics of any value or intensity.

Paste up two sets of analogous colors

Analogous Colors Sample

Analogous Example

Examine the **Amish-Style Scrap Baskets** quilt shown below for a moment. Notice that it contains three analogous colors—blue, purple, and magenta—which are right next to each other at the bottom of the color wheel. Also notice that limiting colors does not necessarily mean that you have to limit the number of fabrics you use. This quilt contains many different fabrics in a variety of values. The colors are mostly grayed in intensity, and the background fabrics are grays and beiges, making a soft, peaceful quilt. The burgundy inner border and the almost royal blue background fabric found in the basket blocks stand out, as these colors are much more intense than many of the others in the quilt.

Amish-Style Scrap Baskets
pieced by Naoko Anne Ito and quilted by Betty Schoenhals

COMPLEMENTARY COLOR SCHEMES

One of the most exciting color concepts is complementary colors, because complementary colors *always* work well together. Every color on the color wheel has one and only one complement, and the two are directly opposite one another on the color wheel. Lay a ruler from the center of any color on the **Color Wheel** (shown at right) across the wheel to the color opposite it to visually study the combinations. The complementary pairs of pure colors are (beginning with yellow and moving clockwise):

yellow and purple
yellow-orange and blue-violet
orange and blue
red-orange and blue-green
red and green
red-violet and yellow-green

Not only does every color on the color wheel have a complement, but the complementary colors physically finish each other. This means that in our eye the two complements provide opposite images that complete the color wheel. For example, red and green are complements; red is a primary color and green is made of equal parts of the other two primary colors, blue and yellow. So together, our eye sees the complete circle of the color wheel, and this provides a comfortable harmony for our eyes. Therefore, complementary colors, if used in good proportions, always make a successful color scheme for a quilt.

Color Wheel

 If a quilt you're working on is starting to look a little less spectacular than you'd hoped, decide what the quilt's main color is, then add a dose of its complement. It can add the spark of color you need to liven up your quilt.

move and vibrate since there won't be a resting place for the viewer's eyes. The **Complementary Colors** illustration below gives an idea of how complements work well together when used in different proportions and how the same color combination is stronger when the complementary colors are used in equal amounts.

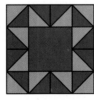 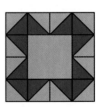 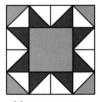

Equal blue and orange   More orange than blue   More orange than blue, plus neutral white

Complementary Colors

Treat Complements Unequally

Although complementary colors look good together, the secret to combining them is to use them in unequal amounts—a lot of one and a little of the other. Used equally, complementary contrast is too strong. Looking at a quilt in which complements are used equally is like looking at vibrant polka dots or checks. The quilt will seem to

To get an idea of how much of each complement to use, look at the proportions of complementary colors used in some printed fabrics. You'll see that a fabric with yellow flowers on a purple background, for instance, contains a lot of purple and little touches of yellow.

Background for Complements

Complements used together are so strong that they often benefit from a neutral background. Consider the lovely red and green on white quilts we frequently see and appreciate. The white softens the two strong colors. So when you put two complements together, consider adding a neutral fabric to soften the combination and increase the impact that each color can make on the quilt. The **Red-and-Green Appliquéd Baskets Quilt** diagram shows how striking this complementary color scheme can be, but notice how much white is used to offset the power of the solid red and green fabrics.

Illustration is based on an antique quilt owned by Cindy Rennels

Red-and-Green Appliquéd Baskets Quilt

A Perfect Accent

When one of the complementary colors is used less frequently, it becomes an accent color. So, knowing what a color's complement is provides you with an instant idea for an accent color in your quilt.

Remember, all values and intensities of two complements are complementary and may be included in your color scheme. Don't limit your thinking and color combinations to pure colors. For example, pink, a light value of red, is a complement of green. So pink and dark forest green can be used to complement one another in a quilt.

The **Pickled Watermelon** quilt shown below is a wonderful example of a quilt that combines two complements, red and green. In this quilt, the red predominates while the green is used in much smaller proportions. The red border increases the amount of red used, and the neutral off-white background softens and breaks up the strong complementary contrast.

Use two complements, a lot of one and a little of the other, on any neutral background, and you will have a stunning quilt. Add some neutral space to soften the contrast.

Pickled Watermelon
made by Julee Prose

Working with Complements

The **Complements** chart below shows three pairs of complementary fabrics. Notice that their intensities and values are varied. In the yellow and purple pair, both fabrics are low in intensity. In the red and green pair, the red is pure while the green is grayed. In the yellow-green and red-violet pair, the red-violet is pure while the yellow-green is a dark value. Even though the values and intensities change from pair to pair, each fabric pair will still work well together because the colors are complementary. From just the three examples shown here, you can begin to imagine the limitless combinations you can create simply by using complementary colors.

Make Complementary Color Schemes

Look through your fabrics and find several pairs of complementary fabrics. While it may be easier to start by pairing pure colors, try to include a wide variety of prints, choosing different values and intensities.

Use the **Complementary Colors Sample** chart below for pasting up your combinations.

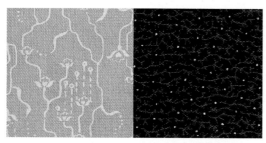

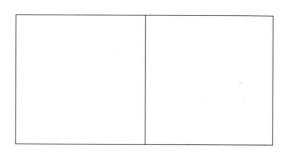

Yellow and purple—both low intensity

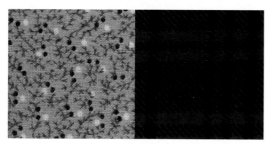

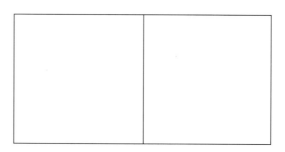

Low intensity yellow-green and pure red

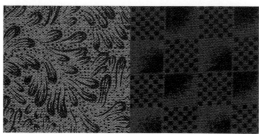

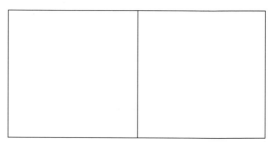

Dark yellow-green and pure red-violet

Complements

Paste up pairs of complementary fabrics

Complementary Colors Sample

WARM AND COOL COLOR SCHEMES

Different colors affect us in ways that relate to our emotional responses. For example, colors are considered to have either a warm or a cool effect. The idea that colors have warmth is the number one concept in your understanding of color because it will affect the design and mood of your quilts.

Look at the **Warm vs. Cool Colors** diagram at right and notice that a straight line drawn across the 12-color wheel will evenly divide the warm colors from the cool ones. The cool colors on the left are the blues and greens of the sky, the sea, and the grass. The warm colors on the right are the yellows, reds, and oranges of fire and the sun.

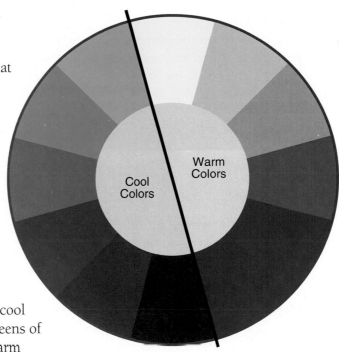

Warm vs. Cool Colors

Color Warmth is Relative

When a color is considered warm or cool, this characterization is made in relation to the other colors used with it. For example, notice that on the color wheel, violet is in the middle between warms and cools. However, violet may appear to be either warm or cool depending on the other colors you combine with it. If you use violet next to red-violet, it will appear to be cooler than the red-violet. On the other hand, when violet is used next to blue-violet, it will appear to be the warmer of the two colors.

Yellow is always a warm color. In fact, it is the strongest color on the color wheel, so it is wise to remember the adage, "A little yellow goes a long way."

Look at the two sets of colors that demonstrate **Relative Color Warmth**, below. The first set—green/blue/violet—is a cool combination, and violet is the warmest color in the set. The second set—violet/red-violet/red—is a warm combination, and the same violet fabric is now the coolest color.

Violet fabric is the warmest of the group

Violet fabric is the coolest of the group

Relative Color Warmth

Warmth is Stimulating

A warm color scheme makes a stimulating quilt. The **Red-and-Orange Baskets** quilt shown below is a good example of a warm color scheme. It is a dynamic quilt because it combines two pure, warm colors (gold and red) on a dark background. The red stands out because it is pure and warm and is used much more in the quilt. The gold triangles stand out even though they are much smaller, because yellow is such a powerful color.

Red-and-Orange Baskets
made by Katie Young and owned by Irene Metz

Cool is Restful

While warm colors stimulate our senses, cool color schemes are soothing. The simple green and white **Antique Double Nine Patch** quilt shown below is striking because of the clear contrast of one medium soft color on white, yet the mood is cool and calm. Any cool color on a white background would provide the same feeling.

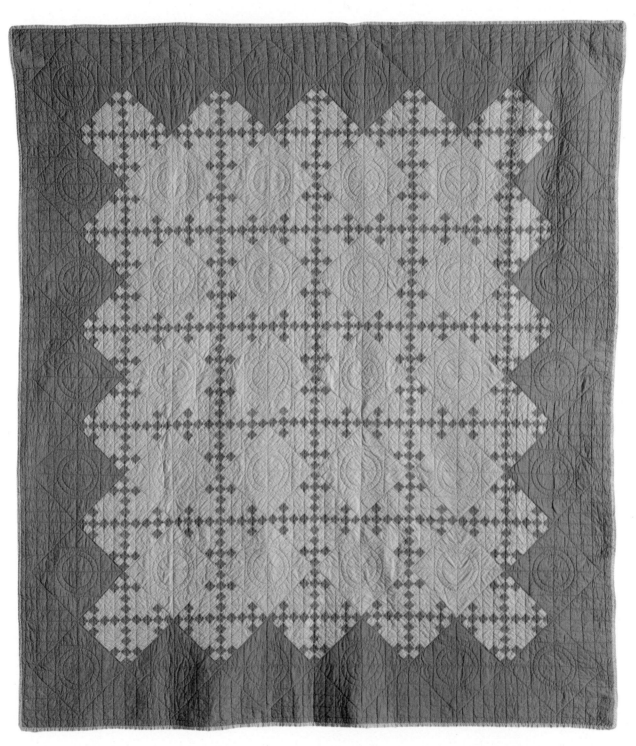

Antique Double Nine Patch
from the collection of Cindy Rennels, maker unknown

Warm and Cool Colors Together

Warm and cool colors used together make a vibrant quilt. When you combine colors that are so different in mood, you can't help but create excitement and movement.

A good example of this theory is shown in the quilt **Summer's End**, shown below. The quiltmaker successfully mixed many warm and cool colors, not to mention a large variety of fabrics.

This quilt is soft in feeling because of its low-intensity grayed plaids and hand-dyed fabrics, yet full of life because it combines warm and cool colors.

Remember that when you use complementary colors you are combining warm and cool, too, which is another reason complementary color schemes are so compelling and exciting.

Summer's End
made by Judy Miller

Make a Warm and Cool Fabrics Sample

Pick a variety of warm and cool fabrics from your collection or scrap basket. Be sure to include different values and intensities. Don't worry about whether the fabrics "go together." They're not a future quilt; they're only samples to remind you of warm and cool colors.

Paste the warm colors together on the left and the cool colors together on the right in the **Warm and Cool Colors Sample** chart, shown below.

Paste up warm colors

Paste up cool colors

Warm and Cool Colors Sample

EARTHTONE COLOR SCHEMES

Earthtones are browns, rusts, and beiges—colors associated with the earth. The rusts are the dark shades of the orange and yellow-orange colors on the right side of the color wheel, which means they are usually warm in feeling.

You've probably noticed that browns do not appear on the color wheel. That's because they are mixtures of many colors on the wheel. They are usually not neutral because they not only contain colors, they are also dark in value, which, added to their color, makes them strong.

The earthtones have been the most popular colors for quiltmakers of all generations. Natural dyes have made beautiful browns and rusts available for many centuries. The invention of commercial dyes in the mid-nineteenth century made earthtone fabrics widely available to quilters, which is one reason we see wonderful antique brown quilts from that period. But earthtones remained a popular color scheme throughout the

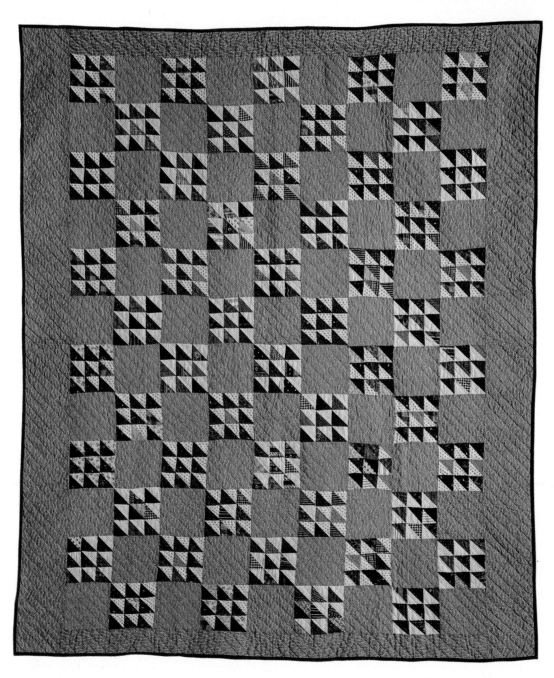

Wild Geese
pieced by an unknown maker, quilted by Shirley McElderry

history of quiltmaking, and today they have become a staple in quilters' color palettes.

One reason for the popularity of earthtones is that they are easy to work with because they are restful and quiet in mood. Even beginners feel comfortable working and experimenting with earthtones. The **Courthouse Steps** quilt shown on page 10 is a glorious study in mid-nineteenth century earthtone fabrics, as is the **Wild Geese** nine-patch variation shown on the opposite page. Both quilts feature simple block patterns that allow the quiltmaker to use many fabrics. Each quilt exudes a calm and restful feeling, despite the combination of dozens of fabrics, because the colors are earthtones.

The **Snowball and Nine Patch** quilt shown below is a contemporary version of an earthtone scrap quilt. Most of the fabrics are browns, and the dark fabrics stand out, creating the design against the light beige background. The touches of color in the green and yellow add spark to the quilt but don't disrupt the overall quiet, earthy feeling.

Snowball and Nine Patch
made by Carolyn Miller

Make An Earthtones Sample

Collect as many samples of earthtone fabrics as you can, including different values and intensities. Remember, the beige quilters' neutrals fit in here, too. Be sure to include a variety of prints, not just solids.

Paste your examples on the **Earthtones Sample** chart, shown below.

Paste up browns, rusts, tans, and quilters' neutrals

Earthtones Sample

SPLIT COMPLEMENTARY COLOR SCHEMES

The split complementary color scheme is a fun one to play and design with. It contains four colors that go together beautifully, including a guaranteed perfect accent. And, while the name may sound a little intimidating, you already know all of the color terms you need to design a quilt using split complements.

First, choose three analogous colors you like, such as blue, blue-violet, and violet. Remember, analogous colors are colors placed next to one another on the color wheel. For the fourth color, look directly across the color wheel from the middle of your three colors. In the blue-to-violet example, you'd find yellow, as shown in the **Split Complementary Colors** swatches on the opposite page. The fourth color may be used in small amounts as an accent color, or it may be used as a major color in the quilt. The split complementary color scheme is easy to plan because it is guided by a formula, but the results won't give away your

secret. No matter which color you start with, your split complementary color scheme will be full of wonderful color play because it will include both analogous and complementary colors.

 *Remember, every value of the four colors you choose will work in the color scheme. You don't need to limit your choices to just the pure color values.*

Make a Split Complementary Sample

Step 1. From among your fabrics find three analogous colors such as red, red-violet, and violet. The fabrics you used earlier as examples of analogous colors will do if you can't find different ones.

Step 2. Use the color wheel on page 13 to find the complement. Remember, it's the color directly opposite the *middle* of your three analogous colors. Paste swatches of each fabric in the **Split Complementary Sample** chart on the opposite page.

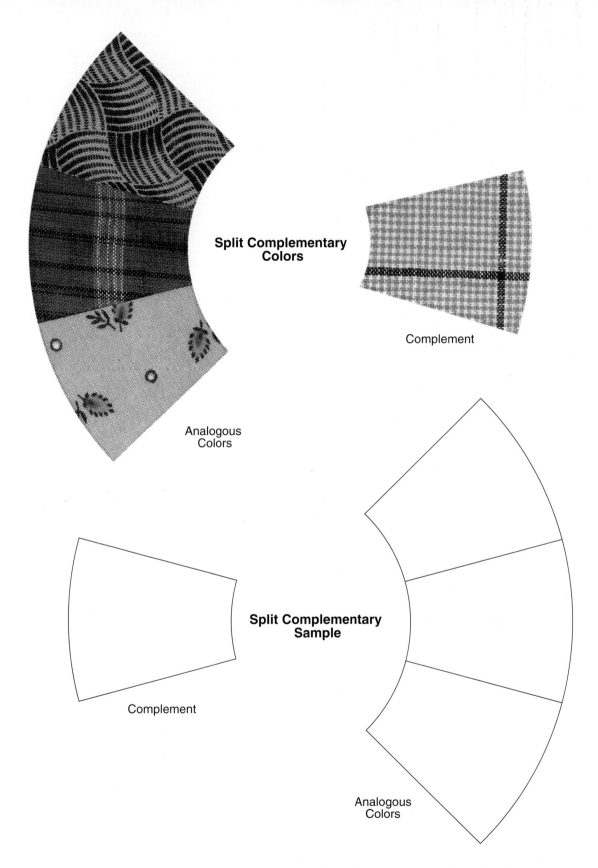

**Split Complementary
Colors**

Complement

Analogous
Colors

**Split Complementary
Sample**

Complement

Analogous
Colors

COLOR WHEEL MASTERY

Now that you've mastered the basic concepts and terms associated with the color wheel itself, you're ready to learn more about how colors behave when they interact with each other. Color contrast and behavior will help you understand why some quilt blocks seem muddled while others work well, and why some quilts seem ordinary while others are truly spectacular.

COLOR
CONTRAST

COLOR CONTRAST

*O*nce *you know how to use the color wheel and understand the terms used to describe it, you are ready to advance your knowledge by learning how the different colors work and behave when used together. Some colors will dominate others, and how you use them together will affect your quilt's visual impact.*

Whether the next quilt you plan to make is a reproduction of a charming antique or your own bright and vivid patchwork interpretation, you'll find that learning to use the principles of color dominance and color contrast effectively will add excitement to your design.

How Colors Behave Together

No, we're not talking about whether they behave or misbehave! The way colors behave has to do with how they interact with each other. Now that you know the basic color terms and you have sought out samples of each from your fabric collection, let's look at fabrics and colors in relation to actual quilts.

Every quilt that contains color is an example of how colors behave together. When you examine quilts in books, magazines, and at quilt shows, try to keep in mind the color terms you have learned, and you'll better understand how colors work together. You'll also have a much easier time creating dynamic color combinations in your own quilts and wallhangings.

COLOR DOMINANCE

Quite simply, different colors behave and affect us differently. When you look at a quilt or anything else with a combination of colors in it, you see some colors first and some later. Why? Because some colors dominate while others fall away or recede.

To describe a color as *dominant* means that it stands out, comes forward, or advances. It catches the viewer's eye first.

Warm Colors Dominate

Generally, warm colors will dominate a quilt. Cool colors do not catch the eye; they recede and act as the background. This means that no matter where on your design you put a cool color, it will tend to fade toward the background, and no matter where you put a warm color, it will catch the viewer's eye first and become the focus or the main design.

To remember this warm vs. cool guideline, think of looking at the sky on a bright summer day. When you look toward the sun, what do you see? The cool blue of the sky, or the hot glow of the bright sun? Although this is a strong example, the theory works for all colors.

Summer Night, shown on page 30, illustrates the dominance of warm colors beautifully. Every block in the quilt is constructed the same way—they're all simple log cabin blocks, as shown below in the **Log Cabin Blocks** diagram. Therefore, in this kind of quilt we can easily see how color and its position controls what we see.

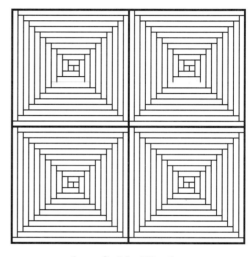

Log Cabin Blocks

In this quilt, the quiltmaker used only two colors: cool blue and warm yellow. Although she used many fabrics in graduated values of each color, most of the fabrics are close to pure in intensity and the overall effect is one of a bright blue and a bright yellow. You can't help but notice how powerful the warm yellow star is. Even though it is a pure color, the powerful yellow advances to the front of the design, leaving the cool blue to automatically recede and become the background of the quilt.

This quilt illustrates perfectly that the quiltmaker controls what we see by where she puts the warm and cool fabrics. Just imagine what the quilt would look like if she had reversed the color placement and the star were blue! There would simply be a big, blue hole in the center of a very yellow quilt.

Summer Night
made by Karen Stone

Pure Colors Dominate

Pure colors are stronger than grayed or toned-down colors, so the intense colors of the color wheel will dominate any grayed colors.

The striking **Grandmother's Flower Garden** quilt, shown on the opposite page, is another example of how color—rather than pieced lines—controls design. In this quilt, the yellow background takes over because it is warm and pure, right off the color wheel—and there's a lot of it.

Remember that yellow is the strongest color on the color wheel. The flowers are usually the dominant design feature in this traditional quilt pattern, but they don't stand a chance here against the powerful yellow background. Most of the flower hexagons are toned-down blue shirtings and feed sacks, and these cool, grayed blues become background to the strong, warm yellow. Notice, however, how the few red hexagons in the quilt do stand out because they, too, are warm and pure.

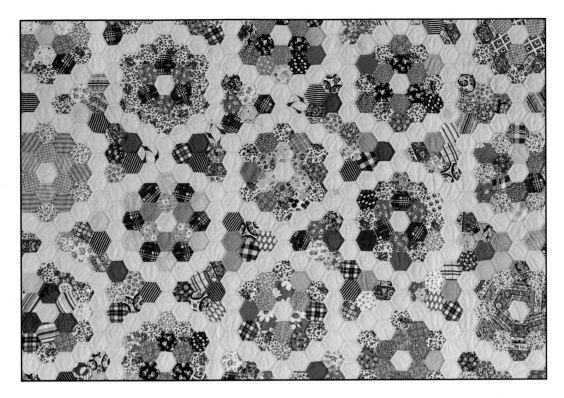

Grandmother's Flower Garden
pieced by Leila Poindexter and hand quilted by Kathryn Jones

Now take a look at how different this quilt would look if the color placements were changed (as in the diagram below). When the flowers are primarily yellow and other warm colors and the background is a cooler color, the quilt leaves the viewer with a completely different impression.

**Grandmother's Flower Garden
with cool background**

Dark Colors Dominate

The third principle of color domination is that · dark colors generally dominate light ones. However, this concept is more flexible than the others. Sometimes light colors stand out against dark backgrounds as a sparkle, especially if there is just a little of the light fabric in the quilt. Most often, though, the dark colors determine the shapes we see in a design.

Again, a Log Cabin quilt is a good example of how this principle works, because the blocks are all the same. This leaves only color to dictate the design. **Paths to the Diamonds,** shown on page 32, is made of a combination of prints that are mostly neutral (black, gray, and white) and red (with a little green in the print). The red fabric stands out because it is pure, dark, and warm, and the black prints also advance because they are very dark, so these are the fabrics you see first. The many grays and light fabrics blend together to form the background.

To test the dark dominance concept, close your eyes for a few seconds and then open them; when you look again you'll see the dark parts of the quilt first. It's not that you don't see the light fabrics, but that the dark colors dominate and control the design.

Paths to the Diamonds
made by Doris Heitman

All Colors Dominate Neutrals

Almost any color is stronger than black, white, gray, or light beige. The definition of a neutral is that it is so weak that it can be dominated, which is why we traditionally use neutrals as background colors. Even black—which is very dark and can dominate light values—can be a background for colors, especially when they are pure and bright.

Take a look at the **Schoolhouse Blocks** illustration at the top of the opposite page, and notice that while all the blocks are the same design, the placement of both light and dark neutrals and colors changes from block to block. You can easily see what a powerful tool color dominance is for creating a whole range of quilt blocks from just one simple block design!

Colors dominate neutrals

Schoolhouse Blocks

DOMINANCE CHANGES

When you combine several colors in a quilt top, you are usually combining a variety of color characteristics, too, such as pure, grayed, dark, light, warm, and cool. In the **Color Dominance** fabric examples below, there are three sets of four fabrics. While some of the fabrics remain constant from one group to another, notice that by changing one of the fabrics in a group we change which fabric is dominant. As the dominant fabric is removed and another fabric is added to the set of swatches, a different fabric becomes the dominant one in the group.

Row 1

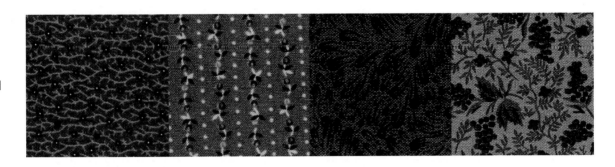

Row 2

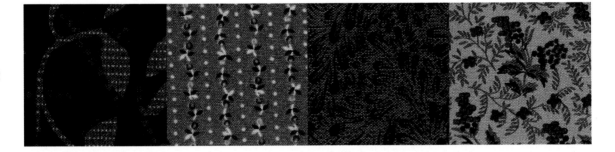

Row 3

Row 1: Blue and purple fabrics are both dark, but purple dominates because it is warmer than the blue fabric.

Row 2: Black and blue fabrics are both dark, but blue dominates because colors dominate neutrals.

Row 3: Gold fabric dominates because it is warm and is closer to a pure color than all other fabrics.

Color Dominance

Experiment with Color Dominance

The best way to learn about how dominance can change is to play with bolts of fabric at the fabric store or with stacks of fabric in your collection.

Step 1. Choose several fabrics you like together, and lay them on the table. Study them to see which fabric or fabrics dominate. Also, decide *why* they dominate.

Step 2. Make some changes to the set, one or two fabrics at a time. Be sure to change the dominant fabrics several times. For example, if the dominant fabric is a pure, warm color, try substituting a pure, cool color to see whether it, too, dominates. Try different values of the dominant colors (such as pink instead of red or rust instead of orange) to see whether they still dominate. By experimenting in this way, you will begin to see how color relationships change as you combine them differently.

If it seems hard to pick out the dominant fabric when they're right in front of you, try standing back about five feet and looking at them again. From that distance, your eye eliminates line and shape and you see only color.

A Lot of One Color Can Dominate

It stands to reason that a lot of any color will make it stand out more within a group of fabrics. Even though the color may not dominate the overall design of the quilt, it will become important in the quilt simply because of its volume.

For example, a large amount of a pale blue used with small bits of a warm red will make what we call a blue quilt. However, the warm color will still be the first element we see and will thus dictate the design of the quilt. A lot of a strong, pure color, even a cool color, will definitely increase its strength and dominance in the quilt.

MAKE SAMPLES OF HOW COLORS BEHAVE

On the following pages are two pairs of quilt block drawings that you can use with your own fabrics to illustrate how colors work and behave to-gether. Trace the blocks to make templates and cut fabric patches to the exact size of the printed blocks. Don't include seam allowances, since these blocks will be pasted together, not sewn. Trace or photocopy the blocks so you can paste several samples onto separate sheets, rather than in your book.

Warm and Cool Colors Sample

Step 1. Select three fabrics that go together—two cool colors and one warm color—to use with the **Bachelor's Puzzle Blocks,** shown on the opposite page. If you want a neutral background fabric, use it as a fourth fabric.

Step 2. Cut pieces for your sample block using templates of the shapes in the block, then lay out a pleasing color design in Block A. When you're satisfied, rub the glue stick over the entire block drawing and paste the fabric to the paper.

Step 3. In Block B, reverse the position of the warm and cool colors. For example, if you used a warm color in the four "X" sections, now use a cool fabric for those pieces. Stand back and notice how different your two blocks look, even though they are made using the same design and fabrics.

If you have fusible web on hand, you may find it easier and neater to work with than glue. Fuse web-bing to the wrong side of the fabrics before you cut out the shapes. Then cut your shapes, finalize your block design, and press your pieces onto a photocopy of the blocks.

Complementary Colors Sample

Step 1. Choose two complementary colors and one neutral fabric to use with **Aunt Sukey's Choice Blocks** on page 36. For Block A, cut fabric pieces to make a block using the two complementary fabrics equally. Arrange your pieces and glue them to the paper. Study this design to see how busy it looks.

Step 2. Use the same two complements in Block B, but use more of one than the other as you lay out your pieces. When you are pleased with the effect, paste the pieces to the paper. Compare the blocks and note how little you used of one complementary color to achieve a pleasing quilt block.

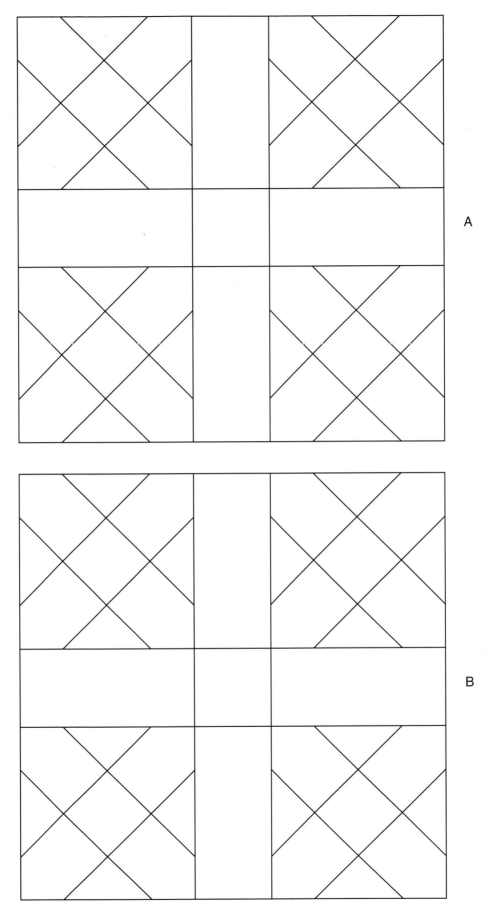

A

B

Bachelor's Puzzle Blocks

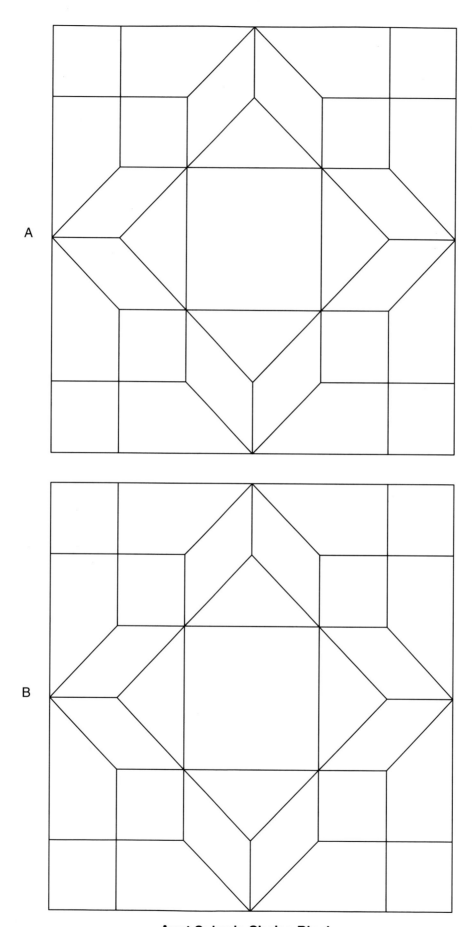

A

B

Aunt Sukey's Choice Blocks

ANALYZING QUILT BLOCKS

Take a moment to look back at the blocks in the Introduction on page iv. Now you know the answer to the questions, "Why does one flower stand out more than the other?" and "Why do the two Joseph's Coat blocks look so different even though they are pieced from the same fabrics?"

One flower block stands out more because one is made of pure red and bright green while the other flower is pale pink and washed-out green. Look at what stands out—the warm and the pure. So in the case of the paler flower, only the warm yellow-orange basket gets noticed.

The Joseph's Coat block has many pieces and the potential for many different designs. Where you put the colors determines which parts of the design will stand out. We used the same fabrics in both blocks: a pure, warm red solid; a black print; a medium, cool blue plaid; and lighter, cool and neutral prints.

In this set of fabrics, it is a safe bet that the pure, warm red and the black will dominate, the medium blue will be next in strength, and the paler fabrics will recede into the background.

This is exactly what happens. We control what design advances in the complicated block by placing the red and black first, then playing with the subordinate colors.

One block is not better than the other, they are just different. Which block design you like best is up to you.

Examine quilts in this and other books for color play, and you'll see that the principles of color dominance are visible, easily identified, and are a tool that you can use in planning your next quilt.

UNDERSTANDING AND USING CONTRAST

One of the easiest ways to enliven a quilt is to include some kind of color contrast. Contrast as a concept is not hard to understand—it is using opposite or different things together. You want contrast in your quilt to make it both interesting and exciting. The quilt pattern itself usually offers a way to play with contrast of line and shape. However, you'll want something interesting happening in color as well as in pattern, since color is the first and most noticeable aspect of any quilt design.

Once you've decided on a quilt pattern or design, the next step is to decide on the colors. As soon as you put two colors together, you are using color contrast—some combinations just provide more contrast than others. In this section, we'll examine the different types of contrast you can use and degrees of contrast you can achieve when planning your quilt color schemes.

ONE COLOR ON WHITE

The simplest color scheme is one color on white. It can be delicate or dramatic in effect and has been used by quilters for generations. Since white is neutral, it will become the background for any colors set against it. If you choose a one-color-on-white scheme and use only a single colored fabric, there is obviously no contrast between colors. The only contrast possible in this color scheme is value contrast. Since the white is light, putting any color against it will provide some degree of contrast. The darker the value, the higher the degree of contrast.

The **Blue-and-White Cherry Baskets** quilt shown below is a lovely example of low contrast in a one-color-on-white quilt. There is no *color contrast* because pale blue is the only color in the quilt. And the blue is so light in value that it is almost as light as the white background and does not offer much *contrast of value*. Thus, the overall effect is delicate and soothing in feel. Pale colors on a white background create the quietest, softest color contrast.

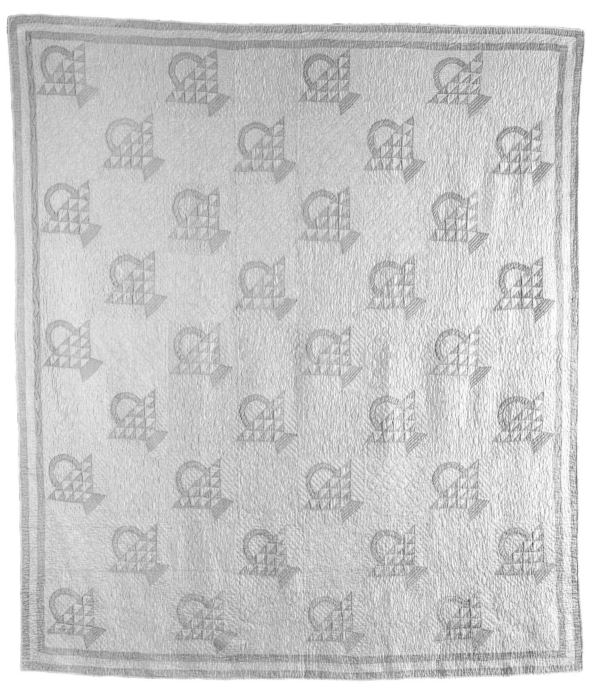

Blue-and-White Cherry Baskets
made by Susan Boyd and owned by her granddaughter, Martha Bastian

Now compare the **Blue-and-White Cherry Baskets** quilt to the red-and-white **Pineapple Log Cabin** quilt, shown below. It, too, is a one-color-on-white quilt, yet it is quite vibrant despite its simplicity of design, fabric, and color scheme. The reason for this is that the quiltmaker used a pure, strong color on white, which creates a very strong contrast of value.

Pineapple Log Cabin
made by an unknown quiltmaker and owned by Edith Leeper

CONTRAST OF VALUE IN ONE-COLOR QUILTS

The red-and-white Pineapple quilt is dramatic because it uses high contrast of value: the solid red is dark set against the white and therefore stands out. The pale blue quilt is quiet because it uses low contrast of value: the solid blue is almost as light in value as the white.

While each of these quilts contains only one solid fabric in the single-color scheme, you can also make a one color quilt using many fabrics. For instance, the red-and-white quilt could just as easily have been pieced using a wide variety of red calicoes on a white background, rather than a single solid red.

As mentioned in the chapter "The Color Wheel," the one-color scheme is an easy one to use if you don't want to worry about combining colors. To avoid the risk of making a dull quilt, a one-color quilt may benefit from some color contrast. So try using as many different fabrics as you can, including fabrics of different scale and type (see page 57) to add textural interest.

When you are mixing lots of prints from the same color family, you'll achieve the strongest contrast of value by placing the lightest and darkest fabrics right next to each other. When you separate dark and light values with medium values, the contrast is softened or diluted.

The **Wild Geese** quilt, shown at left, is a good example of this dilution. It is essentially an all-brown quilt. However, many values of brown are used, from dark browns and deep rusts to light prints, and all are set on the medium value, beige background. Even though this is a peaceful quilt made primarily of quilters' neutrals and earthtones, the varied prints and contrast of value among them provide visual interest.

Examine the blocks closely to see how in some the contrast is very strong, while in others it is lessened because a medium-value brown was used in place of either a dark or a light triangle.

Wild Geese
pieced by an unknown maker, hand quilted and owned by Shirley McElderry

COMPLEMENTARY CONTRAST

When you use two complements together, you are using *complementary contrast*. As mentioned on page 13, complements always look wonderful together and make a strong quilt, but when used equally they seem to vibrate, which makes the quilt hard to look at. Instead, choose one as the predominant color and the other as the accent.

Since *all* values of two complements are complementary, include several values of either or both complements for a more exciting color plan.

A neutral background such as white, black, or beige helps calm down what can be an overpowering color combination. So try controlling the color contrast of two complements you want to use by placing them on a neutral background.

Complementary contrast controls **Honeymoon Cottage**, shown below. This quilt shows successful use of two complements, red and green, with some soft yellow and gray added. The red dominates because it's warm, because it appears in two values, and because it's used in large spaces (such as the roof and chimney). The cool green appears only in the grass, which by comparison is a small space. The house blocks stand out clearly on the neutral white background.

Honeymoon Cottage
made by an unknown quiltmaker and owned by Cindy Rennels

WARM-COOL CONTRAST

There are times when you may not want to include contrast of value; for example, if you are designing an all-pastel quilt. To add interest to such a quilt, try to include both warm and cool colors. When they're mixed, they're always dynamic. It doesn't matter what values you include—they can be all dark or all light. Just the fact that the colors themselves are so different enlivens your quilt.

Warm-cool contrast is one of the most fun types of contrast to play with because it allows you to use any colors you want as long as you include some from each side of the color wheel.

Mountain Mirage, shown below, is a study of warm/cool contrast. A wide variety of colors and values move from warm to cool in this restful quilt. The great variety of color doesn't overwhelm the quilt because the changes in value are gradual and give the viewer's eyes a direction in which to travel.

Mountain Mirage
made by Kathryn Kuhn

PURE COLORS TOGETHER

The strongest color contrast is between the strongest colors—the 12 pure colors on the color wheel. Using any number of these pure colors together will assure a vibrant quilt.

Red, White, and Blue, shown below, is just such a vibrant quilt, with three pure colors from the color wheel set on a white background. Not only are these three colors pure, but they are the primary colors out of which all other colors are mixed. Using the three primary colors alone could be quite overpowering, so the neutral white was needed to define the quilt's design. Notice how the yellow squares jump out even though they are small, because yellow is the strongest color.

Red, White, and Blue
probably made by Lillie Miller Rohrbach and owned by Lucille Powell

Amish Easter Baskets, a bright, cheerful quilt, Crayola-like in feeling, is another example in which pure colors are combined for a striking effect (see the photo below). Red, blue, and green right off the color wheel control the traditional design. Again, notice that the high color contrast is softened by a neutral white background.

Amish Easter Baskets
made by Elsie Vredenberg and owned by the Museum of the American Quilter's Society in Paducah, Kentucky

CONTRAST OF INTENSITY

When pure colors are mixed with grayed colors, the result is a *contrast of intensity*. The pure colors stand out, while the grayed colors recede. This combination happens naturally when you combine a great number of colors and fabrics in a scrap or charm quilt, such as in **Simply Charming**, shown below. It's full of variety in fabric and color. Notice how the pure yellows, reds, purples, and yellow-greens advance while the other fabrics recede.

Not only do some colors advance and others recede, but in this quilt the intensity of the colors changes the design we see. For example, in some sections of the quilt, the patches combine to form six-pointed stars. Yet in other areas, the less intense color fabrics are arranged so that we see a more traditional Tumbling Blocks arrangement. All the patches are exactly the same size and shape; it's the color play that dictates the design. What do you see when you look at **Simply Charming?**

Simply Charming
made by Edith Zimmer

COMBINING DIFFERENT KINDS OF CONTRAST

Usually a quilt contains more than one kind of contrast. For example, when you use pure colors on white, you are automatically using contrast of value, too. And remember the color wheel on page 17, where the wheel is divided in half, separating the warm colors from the cool ones? That means complementary contrast always includes warm-cool contrast because any two complements are across the color wheel from one another.

The exuberant **6 ÷ 3 = 5** hexagonal quilt, shown on page 46, incorporates all kinds of color contrast. It uses all the colors of the color wheel in many values, including the pure version and grayed versions of each. It includes warm colors and cool ones, and emphasizes the warm-cool contrast by the placement of the hexagons. The quilt relies on color contrast to make it bright.

The many kinds of color contrast mix with the other elements of quilt design—blocks, sashing, borders, and binding—to create lively quilts. You don't always have to think in terms of color contrast first. But color contrast will be there; it will affect the quilt. It is an idea to which you can turn when you want a way to add a bit of life your quilt. Color contrast in quilts, as in life, is invigorating.

6 ÷ 3 = 5
made by Edith Zimmer

BACKGROUNDS AFFECT COLOR CONTRAST

When you consider which colors to use in a quilt, you need to consider background color, too. In order to stay in the background and not draw attention to itself, the fabric you choose must be neutral or a receding color.

BLACK AS BACKGROUND

Black is a wonderful background for the powerful, pure colors. It brings out their vibrance. In the Amish **Robbing Peter to Pay Paul** quilt, shown below, you can see how the black background enlivens the pure colors.

Now take a look at a few more sample block diagrams to see how the pure colors, and even some darker or grayed ones, stand out against the black background. The black fabric makes the pure, vibrant colors sing.

Oklahoma Nine Patch

Roman Stripe

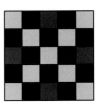
Irish Chain

Robbing Peter to Pay Paul
made by Becky Herdle

WHITE AS BACKGROUND

White has the complete opposite effect on colors when it's used as a background. It softens colors and makes a more delicate background. Sometimes it even dulls colors. When you decide to place colors on a white background, think about contrast of value, too. Light colors, even warm ones like yellow, will blend into a white background, as you can see in the **Scrap Baskets with Nine-Patch Sashing** quilt, shown below. The dark baskets show up well, but the light fabrics and the prints with white backgrounds have less contrast of value. Although you can see them up close because they have some color, from a distance they are very close in value to the white quilt background, which makes for a quiet, soothing quilt.

Scrap Baskets with Nine-Patch Sashing
made by Wilma Sestric

BLACK AND WHITE TOGETHER

Black and white placed right next to each other are always dynamic because they create the ultimate contrast of value, the darkest dark against the lightest light. They may also be used together as background. **Barn Raising Pinwheels**, shown below, and **Oklahoma Nine Patch**, shown on page 50, both use both black and white as background. The high contrast between the black and white rows enhances the action of the many prints, most of which are bright and pure in color. Black, white, and pure colors always make for a dynamite color combination.

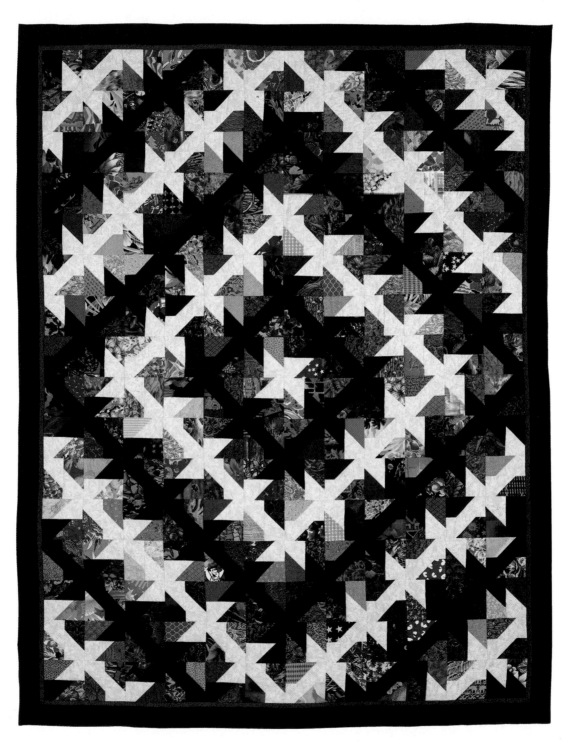

Barn Raising Pinwheels
pieced by Barbara Berliner and machine quilted by Cathy Sexton

Oklahoma Nine Patch
made by Carolyn Miller

GRAY AS BACKGROUND

Gray is quieting and softening wherever you put it. It is by definition medium in value, so its effects are medium, too. It recedes, it calls no attention to itself, and it is, therefore, the ultimate neutral. Look at the **Amish-Style Scrap Baskets** quilt on page 12. In this quilt, the gray background allows the blocks to stand out even though they are made of soft grayed colors themselves. They would have been lost on a black background (traditional for an Amish-style quilt) because, although neutral, the black is powerful in value and could easily overpower and deaden the low-intensity colors of the baskets.

MUSLIN AND LIGHT BEIGE AS BACKGROUND

This **Postage Stamp Baskets** quilt contains mostly low intensity fabrics on a muslin background (see photo below). Choosing a sashing for these blocks could easily have presented a problem to the quiltmaker. Too strong a sashing would have taken over and dominated the delicately colored blocks. Too light a sashing would have been too dull and faded into the muslin background. The grayed-green sashing is a perfect choice. It provides a soft contrast to the muslin background yet recedes enough to allow the colors in the baskets to stand out.

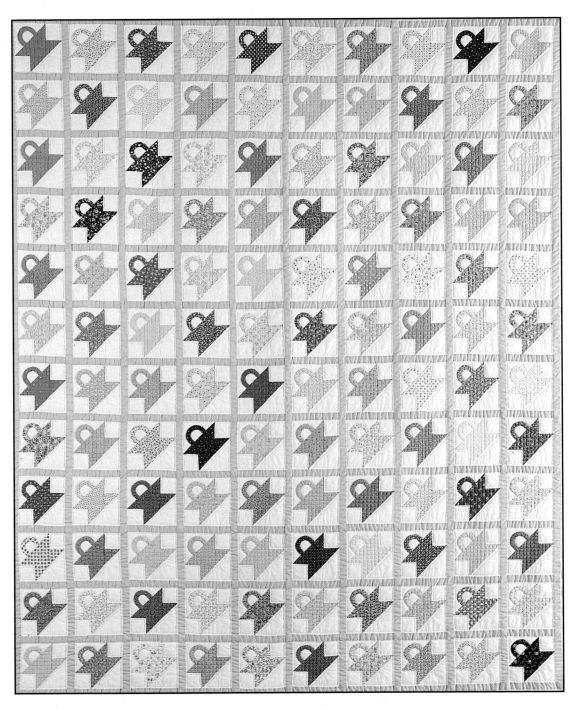

Postage Stamp Baskets
made by Martha Bastian

My Cabin Made of Logs, shown below, is essentially a red, white, and blue quilt, a warm and cool color combination that is always strong.

By replacing the traditional white background with beige, however, the quiltmaker has softened the high contrast of the usual red-and-navy-on-white color scheme and produced a more mellow quilt. Notice that although the background contains many fabrics, they are the same color and are close in value, so overall the background remains beige.

You can add interest to your quilt's background by using a variety of prints or plaids, as shown in **My Cabin Made of Logs**. *As long as the fabrics are basically the same color, you'll have the color effect you want, but the different prints will add a bit of spice to the design.*

My Cabin Made of Logs
made by Jane Graff

Blue as Background

Blue is the background color of our lives. It is always above us in the sky, varying day to day and season to season from clear, bright blues, to grayed blues, to midnight blues. It is also a cool color that recedes when mixed with other colors. Thus, it is a perfect background for quilts of all kinds. In its pure version, it was used successfully in **Summer Night,** shown on page 30.

In **Silver Anniversary,** shown below, blue is used in a grayed form. There are two background fabrics in the quilt: beige and silvery blue. The pieced rings in bright, warm pinks and roses stand out against both background fabrics. But by mixing the gray-blue and muslin backgrounds, the quiltmaker creates a secondary design for the blocks within the background, giving the quilt drama and presence.

Silver Anniversary
designed by Annie Segal, pieced by Penny Wolf, and machine quilted by Jonna Castle

Combining Colors and Prints

Up until now, we've been discovering how colors work together to provide impact. From complementary colors, to color dominance, to choosing background colors, we've been focusing strictly on color itself. However, unless you are making an Amish-style quilt or a traditional red-and-green appliqué quilt, you probably aren't limiting your fabric choices to just solid colors. Wonderful prints, plaids, and paisleys are all available to quiltmakers, and understanding how the printed designs affect the impact of color in quilts is important. In the next section, "Using Prints of Yesterday and Today," we will introduce a variety of printed fabric styles and show you how to use fabrics and colors effectively to plan your own quilt color schemes.

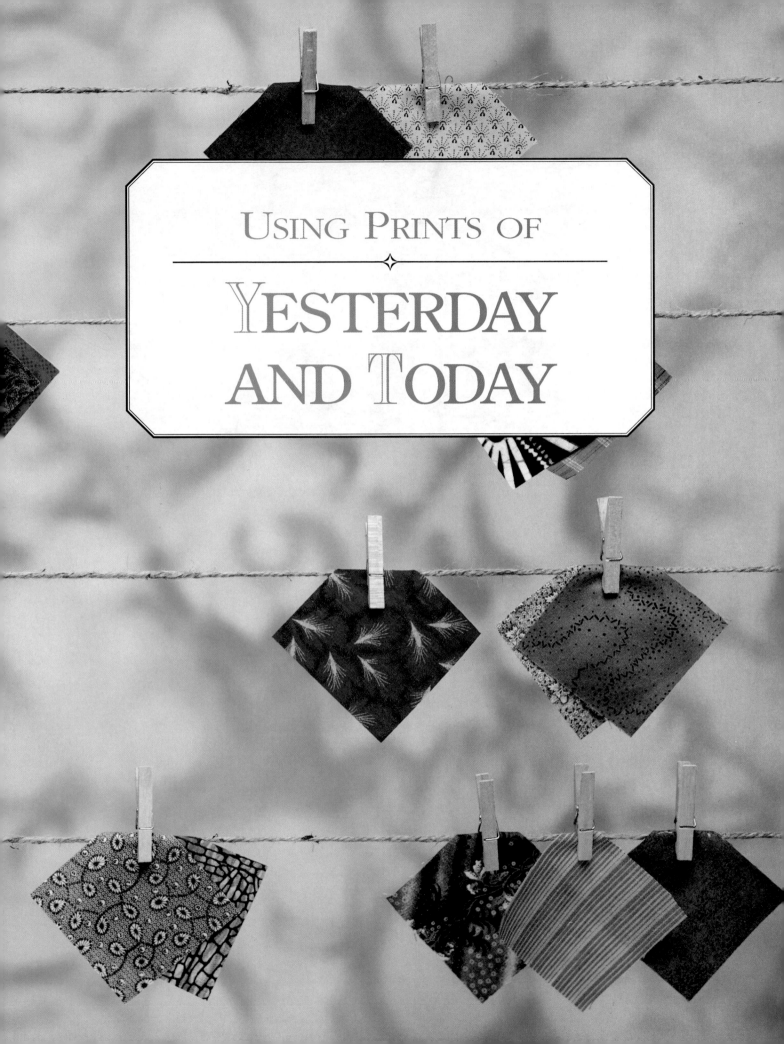

Using Prints of
Yesterday and Today

USING PRINTS OF YESTERDAY AND TODAY

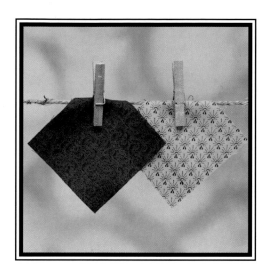

An affinity for fabric is the reason many quilters make quilts. And unlike our grand-mothers and great grandmothers, we don't have to rely on leftover bits of fabric from the clothing we make to piece our quilt tops. Instead, we have almost unlimited fabric choices, ranging from traditional calicoes and homespun plaids to glittery metallics and mottled hand-dyed cottons.

To keep our interest piqued, fabric designers change the colors and patterns from season to season and year to year. Even though available colors and designs may change, fabrics continue to be made in standard, definable prints.

As a quiltmaker, it is important to recognize the different types of prints and to be sure to include all kinds in your collection. It's not just the color that makes a quilt exciting; the creative blending of lots of different types of fabrics also contributes to the visual impact.

Working with Printed Fabrics

Quite often, beginning quiltmakers look at a quilt top they've completed and wonder why it isn't as exciting as they imagined it would be when they first planned the colors and selected the fabrics. In many cases, the reason is not the colors used but the lack of variety in the printed fabrics. Too many medium-size floral prints or an over-abundance of pin dots and other miniature-scale prints can lead to a lackluster quilt.

It's easy to see why we as quiltmakers could fall into this trap. After all, we wouldn't dream of wearing a polka-dot blouse with a plaid skirt. However, fabrics are used differently in a quilt, so we need to learn how to combine a variety of prints for an effective quilt design, not based on fashion concerns! If you've ever hesitated to use paisleys, plaids, and polka dots in the same quilt, keep reading. By the end of the chapter, you'll see why more fabric variety leads to livelier quilts.

Recognizing Types of Prints

Prints come in different sizes and styles. Some are monochromatic, and some contain a variety of colors. Some patterned fabrics aren't even printed, they have their designs woven right into them. Woven plaids and stripes are easy to spot, since they look the same on both sides. Regardless of what type of printed or woven pattern you prefer, what's important in quiltmaking is how you combine different prints together.

By mixing different styles and sizes of prints, you'll be adding dimension, interest, and excitement to the overall look of your finished quilt.

In this section we'll discuss the characteristics of print types and show you examples of each. We've left space next to our examples for you to paste up samples from your own collection of fabrics. If you don't want to glue directly into your book, photocopy these pages or just keep a notebook with a page for samples of each type of print.

This exercise will give you a chance to review your fabric collection and will call to your attention what kinds of prints you like best. It may also suggest areas where you need to add variety to your collection, so keep a notebook handy to jot down your fabric shopping list.

Kinds of Prints

Floral: A floral print, as the name implies, contains flowers. This is the largest and most varied category of quilt fabric. Flowers may be tossed randomly over a fabric or appear in a definite direction; they may be widely spaced or close together. Notice, too, that floral prints can contain lots of color contrast or just a little, and they can also provide a great deal of or very little contrast in value, as shown below.

Floral Prints

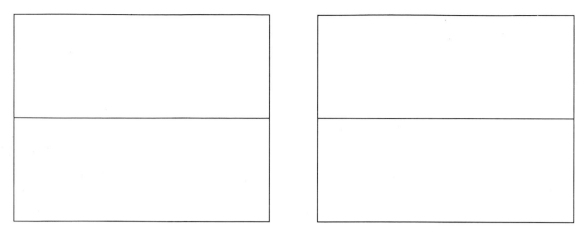

Floral Print Samples

Geometric: Geometric prints are designs based on geometric shapes such as circles, squares, and triangles, as well as checks, stripes, and plaids, as shown below. Patterns may be all over, directional, widely spaced, or packed, just as in florals. And again, the degree of contrast within the design, both in color and value, can vary greatly.

Geometric is the one category where you can have a design woven into the fabric, such as a stripe, check, or plaid, rather than printed on top of the fabric. The benefit of a woven fabric is that the design appears on both sides, so you can use either side without worrying about sewing right sides together.

Evenly spaced geometric

Check

Plaid

Random geometric

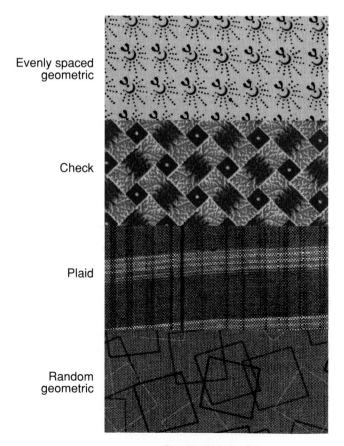

Geometric Prints

Geometric Print Samples

Using Prints of Yesterday and Today

Conversational: A conversational or novelty print depicts a real thing. Celestial prints were popular in the nineteenth century, as were prints showing horses and riding accessories such as saddles, horse shoes, bits, and reins. Prints of games and toys were popular for children's clothing in the early twentieth century and eventually worked their way into patchwork.

Today, you can find examples of all these conversational prints, as many fabric manufacturers are producing fabrics to simulate novelty fabrics of earlier times, as shown below.

Conversational Prints

Conversational Print Samples

Abstract: Abstract prints are prints that do not portray a specific recognizable shape, unlike the floral, geometric, and conversational prints already shown. Abstract prints include (but certainly aren't limited to) designs that swirl, are irregularly shaped, or look sponge painted or hand painted, as shown in the fabric swatches below. Paste your sample abstract prints on page 60.

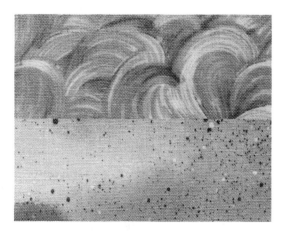

Abstract Prints

Abstract Print Samples

Ethnic: Prints with a foreign or exotic feeling, as shown below, are referred to as ethnic prints. These are Western interpretations of the fabrics of different regions of the world, such as African and Native American prints, Dutch wax prints, Indonesian batiks, Egyptian designs, and others.

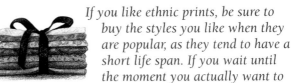 *If you like ethnic prints, be sure to buy the styles you like when they are popular, as they tend to have a short life span. If you wait until the moment you actually want to use one, you may not be able to find the style print you're looking for.*

African print

Dutch wax print

Indonesian batik

Japanese print

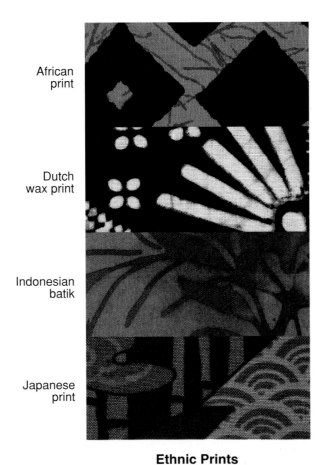

Ethnic Prints

Ethnic Print Samples

SCALES OF PRINTS

The size of the design printed on the fabric is referred to as the print *scale*. It is important that quilters understand the concept of scale, because the use of different scale prints gives impact to quilt design. Too often, quiltmakers limit themselves to small-scale calicoes, especially when first starting out. Instead of thinking small, think about variety. Our quilting forebears used a great variety of print sizes, and that partly accounts for the depth and richness of their quilts.

Many quilters don't choose a variety of prints for a quilt simply because they only want to include fabrics that they truly love. And, quite simply, they tend to like the same style of print, whether it be small-scale geometrics or medium-scale florals. When quilters shop for fabrics they are drawn to the same types of fabrics repeatedly. To avoid the trap of using the same scale of prints, select fabrics based on what they will do for your quilt, not on how well they would fit in your wardrobe. Remember, you'll be cutting each fabric into small pieces so it won't end up looking like the huge print you see on the bolt anyway!

To see how different scales of prints work together, cut a square- or triangle-shaped window in the center of a piece of white paper. Take it to the fabric store with you and lay it over the fabrics you select to see how they will look when cut into those shapes. Don't be afraid to add variety to your quilt. If you have the right colors but your selection of fabrics still seems less than exciting, spice up your project by changing the print scales.

Print Scale

Print Scale Samples

Color Contrast within Fabrics

Printed fabrics exemplify the same color principles that were discussed in the chapter "Color Contrast." For instance, once you add a pink rosebud with green leaves to a yellow background, you've changed the appearance of solid yellow because other colors have been introduced.

The most important thing to remember about color and fabric, however, is that color is a long-distance illusion. Even a fabric with many colors in it will appear to be predominantly one color; in this example, the rosebuds and leaves won't matter. In order to tell a fabric's true color, stand back to view the fabric. From a few feet away the blend of colors will probably look different from how it does up close. Remember, you will be using tiny pieces mixed with other colors, and that, too, will affect how the fabric looks. The tiny specks of buds and leaves will not be visible from a distance, and the colors will blend into one.

In this section, we will explore the variety of contrasts available in different types of prints—from high-contrast complements to very subtle shading nuances.

 *Don't be overly concerned about matching every color in every print you select. It really doesn't matter whether a tiny sprig of green in a floral print matches the greens in the other prints you are considering. All greens will blend into the other colors when you view them from a distance.*

Solid Prints

Solids, of course, are easily classified by color. *Solid prints* are low-contrast prints on a color, usually two values of a color or black on a color. They provide interest upon close-up viewing but look like solids from a distance.

Today, even the traditional muslin (bleached or unbleached) is being supplemented by white-on-white prints, and manufacturers are providing quilters with more and more choices of neutral tone-on-tone prints. They're easy to work with because they definitely recede into the background as muslin does, but they offer a bit of variety upon close-up viewing, as shown in **Solid Prints,** below. Paste your samples of solid prints in the spaces provided at the top of the opposite page.

 If you are used to using some solids in your patchwork because you find it difficult to mix prints, try replacing the solids with solid prints. While a solid print won't offer a lot of contrast, it will add more close-up interest to your quilt.

Solid Prints

Solid Print Samples

COMPLEMENTARY COLORS IN FABRICS

When prints have several colors in them, you can see that the fabric designers used the standard theories of color contrast within the printed fabrics. Complementary contrast and warm-cool contrast, both shown below, are popular in fabrics.

Because such fabrics contain high contrast and often a variety of colors, they're sometimes considered busy and hard to use. But their busyness is what makes them interesting. Try using them for larger quilt patches where the print can fill the space with detail, or use them as the basic fabric from which you pull other colors for the quilt.

Complementary Contrast in Prints

Complementary Contrast Print Samples

ANALOGOUS COLORS IN FABRICS

Analogous colors are also frequently used together in prints. They make beautiful color combinations in fabric just as they do in quilts. Notice how pleasing and soothing the analogous color fabrics shown below are to the eye.

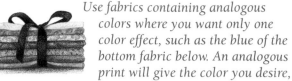

Use fabrics containing analogous colors where you want only one color effect, such as the blue of the bottom fabric below. An analogous print will give the color you desire, but make your quilt appear richer from a distance because of the subtle additions of closely related colors.

Analogous Contrast in Prints

Analogous Colors Print Samples

VARY YOUR FABRICS

Include a variety of prints in any quilt you make—variety is the spice of quilts as well as the spice of life! If you include fabrics of different color contrasts, kinds, and scales of print, you will have an interesting quilt, as exemplified in the portion of the **Scrap Half Log Cabin** quilt shown at right. The quilt contains stripes, geometrics, high contrast fabrics, and beige-on-white tiny floral, all in scraps.

Scrap Half Log Cabin
made by Sharyn Craig

Identifying and Using Prints of the Past

Many prints and fabric types are identified with particular periods in quiltmaking history. Even though they were not designed particularly for quilters, they were used extensively in quilts and can actually help us date antique quilts.

Today, reproduction fabrics are being made that enable us to re-create the looks of time-honored antique quilts. It is useful to know some of the kinds of fabrics found in quilts of different historical periods and how to identify them in both antique quilts and reproduction fabrics. With this knowledge you can replicate the look of an heirloom quilt if you want to. Here are some of the most important styles of prints and the periods in which they were most popular. Using any of the fabrics from these periods or combining them is what will give your quilt an historic look.

Calicoes

The calicoes quilters are so fond of have been available since the mid-nineteenth century. The word *calico* originally referred to tightly woven cotton cloth imported from Calicut, India, but it soon became the name for the brightly colored, small-scale florals, shown below, that we think of as traditional in quilts. Calicoes were widely avail-

able and found their way into quilts as well as clothing. Even today, with literally thousands of bolts of new and vibrant fabrics lining the shelves of quilt shops, calicoes remain a staple to quiltmakers.

Use calicoes sparingly. These safe, predictable fabrics often look solid from a distance, so they don't give your quilt as much texture and pattern as other types of prints would.

Double Pinks or Cinnamon Pinks

Many variations of these small-scale pink-on-pink or floral prints, shown below, were printed from the 1860s through the 1920s. Inexpensive and widely available in stores throughout the United States, they were often used in quilts and are enjoying a new wave of popularity since reproductions are available today.

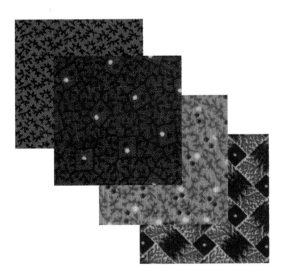

Double Pinks

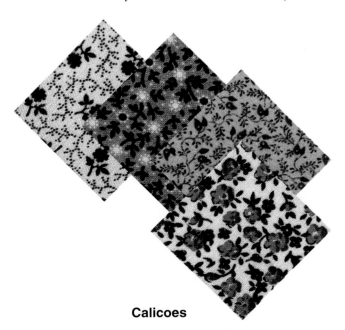

Calicoes

Double pinks are always bright in color, so use them sparingly, too. They are very powerful, so a small amount can make quite a statement.

FEEDSACK CLOTH

During the Great Depression, feedsacks were printed with brightly colored, cheerful florals and conversational prints, as shown below. Clever homemakers didn't let the precious fabric go to waste. They used the sacks to make clothing for their families and to patch into quilt tops. When manufacturers realized that their printed sacks were being used for home sewing, they had them printed with feed company labels that would wash out so every bit of the precious fabric could be used.

Feedsack Prints

Feedsack fabrics were loosely woven and coarse compared to today's quilting cottons, so they are not good fabrics for a quilt that will get a lot of use. Reserve authentic feedsack fabrics for a special project or choose reproductions, which are printed on high-quality cotton.

GREENS

Green fabrics were popular in the early nineteenth century, but they had one disappointing feature—they faded more than any other color. At that time, green was printed by over-dyeing, combining yellow and blue. Both colors faded, often at different rates, which accounts for antique quilts with appliquéd leaves that have turned tan, yellow, or blue, or sometimes blotchy combinations of these three. These leaves were probably originally green. According to Barbara Brackman in her book, *Clues in the Calico*, late nineteenth century and early twentieth century greens "could also fade away completely, leaving ghostly white leaves and stems among the still-bright flowers."

Acid or apple green was a yellow-green calico that frequently included black and yellow in the print. Sometimes this color is also referred to as poison green, since it was the color of arsenic. Acid green is found in quilts from the mid-nineteenth century, but when these quilts were sewn the greens were probably not as yellow as they appear today. Prints of this color are also available in reproductions today, as shown below.

Acid green is very strong because it's so close to yellow, so some quilt-makers find it hard to use. Try small bits of it where you want a very bright color, or incorporate it into a project that you want to replicate the look of a nineteenth century quilt.

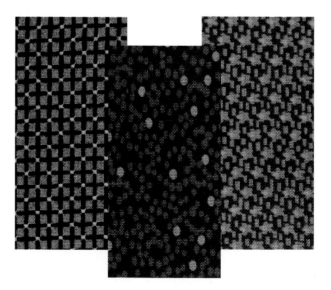

Acid Green Prints

Depression green is a pale, bluish green that was quite popular from the Great Depression years up until the 1950s. Unlike acid green or other shades of green, it was usually used as a solid rather than in prints, as shown below.

Depression Green

For an authentic 1920s look, use depression green in sashing and borders around appliqué or a patchwork design full of color.

SHAKER GRAYS AND HALF-MOURNING PURPLES

These dark-hued calicoes (shown below and at right) were available throughout the nineteenth century and were widely used in quilts of the time. They were originally designed to be "worn by widows who had passed out of the stage of mourning proper, when they were expected to wear black… [and they] were favored by practical rural working women, not necessarily bereaved, because their speckled textures and dark colors required less frequent laundering," according to Susan Meller and Joost Elffers in *Textile Designs*. Reproduction Shaker grays and half-mourning purples such as the swatches shown below are popular with quilt-makers today.

Shaker grays and half-mourning purples make great neutrals. Even though purple is a strong color, the dull purples are surprisingly good neutrals, and the prints provide visual texture to the background.

Shaker Grays

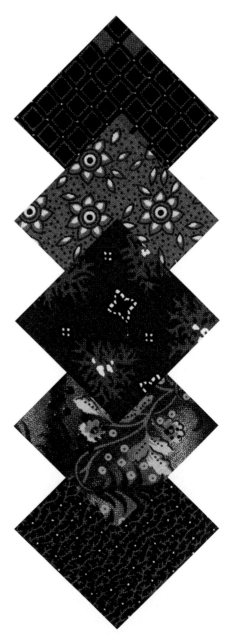

Half-Mourning Purples

INDIGOS

The word *indigo* refers to the vivid, deep blue fabric dyed from the indigo plant. In the nineteenth century, indigo prints in blue and white, several values of blue, or blue, yellow, and white were widely available and frequently used in quilts. Indigos are one of the few types of antique fabrics that maintain their color. This is because the indigo dyes were so stable. Today, quiltmakers can find reproductions of typical indigo prints, as shown below, but actual indigo dyes cannot be used to make these fabrics in the United States because when they are released during the manufacturing process they cause water pollution.

Because indigos are very close to being pure in color, they're very strong colors. They will dominate a quilt, so use them in the parts of your design that you want to emphasize.

MADDERS

Madder is a vegetable dye derived from the root of the madder plant. It produces many different browns, rusts, oranges, purples, and reds, as shown below. Madder-dyed fabrics are seen in most quilts from the eighteenth and nineteenth centuries, because madder was the most common dye of the era.

Madder Prints

Indigos

NEATS

Commonplace in the second half of the nineteenth century, *neats* were small scale, simple designs printed in only one or two colors, as shown below. They could be either floral or geometric, and they were a staple fabric of the time. Neats were usually brown, red, blue, or black figures on a white background, or the reverse. Many of this style print were manufactured because they were inexpensive to print. They were used primarily in clothing such as blouses, shirts, and pajamas, but many of them made their way into quilts.

SHIRTINGS: PLAIDS, STRIPES, AND CHECKS

Popular throughout the nineteenth and twentieth centuries as clothing, the pale blue and brown shirting stripes, plaids, and checks, shown below, became widely available in the late nineteenth and early twentieth centuries. Shirtings were commonly used in turn-of-the-century scrap quilts, and are popular again today.

One way to add a bit of extra texture in you next scrap quilt is to use one or several light-color shirting fabrics for the backgrounds of your quilt blocks.

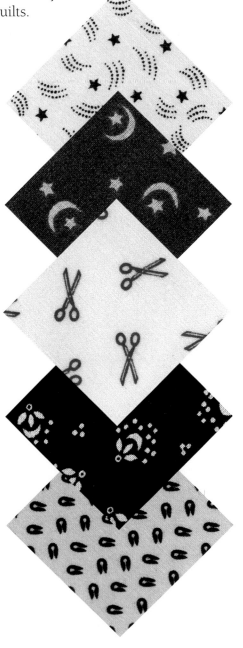

Neats

Shirtings

OMBRÉS

Also called *rainbow* or *fondu prints,* the *ombrés* contain a print over a background that shades and blends gradually from one value to another or from one color to another. These fabrics were popular from the 1840s through the 1850s and are seen frequently in quilts of that period. Reproductions, such as those shown below, are especially popular with the many quiltmakers interested in quilt history.

TURKEY REDS

Turkey red refers to a deep, rich, scarlet red. These wonderful and complicated prints became commercially available in the early 1800s. French Provincial in style, Turkey red prints contain wild, large florals and floral stripes. They are primarily red and feature black, blue, yellow, and white. Solid cloth in the same rich red was used in many quilts of the nineteenth century, and to quilters the term "Turkey red" has come to mean any print or solid in this deep, rich, slightly rusty red. Turkey red is a favorite of quiltmakers because no matter how you use it, it's always dramatic.

Ombré Prints

Turkey Red Prints

Re-creating the Look of Bygone Eras

In addition to recognizing the specific types of fabric associated with quilts of particular historical eras, there are other key characteristics that tie in with specific time periods. In this section we will discuss how to replicate the quilts of different eras by including significant colors, prints, and patterns. For each era listed below, I've also provided information regarding typical fabrics, colors, backgrounds, block designs, and styles of quilting used in quilts of bygone eras.

Mid-nineteenth century red and green quilts
Mid-nineteenth century scrap quilts
Late nineteenth century red and white quilts
Turn of the century scrap quilts
1920s pastel quilts
1920s Lancaster County Amish quilts
1930s depression quilts

Although we are concentrating on making quilts look old through color and fabric, you can more closely replicate a particular style of quilt by using the same types of quilt blocks, quilting motifs, and fabrics popular at a particular time.

Some of the quilt examples that follow are authentic antiques, while others are contemporary quilts that really do capture the flavor of earlier quiltmaking eras.

The Mid-Nineteenth Century Red-and-Green Quilts

Fabrics: Both solids and calicoes

Colors: Turkey red, green, acid green, tan, gray-blue, or yellow (Green often faded to tan or blue, thus they are frequently seen in antique red-and-green quilts from this period. Yellow is frequently seen if the design required a third color.)

Background: Bright white or muslin

Quilting: Close, tiny, and elaborate in design

Blocks: Many red-and-green quilts of this period were florals, either appliqué or a combination of appliqué and patchwork. Album and Baltimore album quilts were essentially red-and-green quilts with many colors added in much smaller doses.

*This **Red-and-Green Appliquéd Baskets** quilt, owned by Cindy Rennels, is believed to have been made between 1860 and 1870 and is typical of mid-nineteenth century red and green florals. It contains Turkey red, green, and yellow (possibly discolored green from which the blue dye faded) fabrics on a white background. The green has faded to a tan that is visible and attractive. It is filled with close background grid quilting typical of the mid-nineteenth century. The flowers in the baskets or urns are cockscombs, a motif popular during that era.*

Making Quilts That Look Antique

With all of the reproduction fabrics on the market today, it's easy to make a brand new quilt that looks like a quilt from your favorite bygone era. But the one thing that may be missing is the faded, soft, well-used look of a real antique. Part of the charm of the antique originals is the yellowed look of age or the faded softness of their colors. Sometimes it's nice to make quilts that capture the look of well-used and much-washed utilitarian quilts. Here are some pointers on making a new quilt with a built-in old look.

Yellow-Beiges and Faded Fabrics

Begin to search for and collect yellow-beiges and faded-looking fabrics. The swatches shown at right will give you an idea of the type of print and color to look for. There are many on the market, often scorned for their dullness and lack of brilliance. Collect them to use in antique-looking quilts. They can easily look as if they were once whites which have yellowed, and they would look perfect in an "old" quilt.

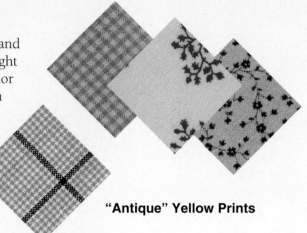

"Antique" Yellow Prints

Shirting Fabrics

Shirting fabrics in pale stripes and plaids have a faded look, and many grayed fabrics look as if they could be faded versions of vivid originals. Also, examine the backs of current fabrics. Many of them are softened echoes of the print on the front, so using the wrong side can simulate the effects that time has on fabric, as shown below.

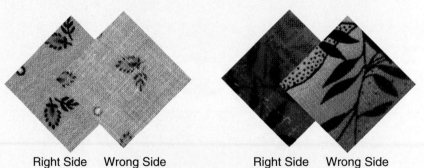

Right Side   Wrong Side   Right Side   Wrong Side

Wrong sides of fabrics look faded

Make Old-Looking Fabric

You can make your own old-looking fabric. Over-dyeing fabric softens the brilliance of a color and makes it look yellowed with age. Jane Nehring, who wrote the article "Aging Gracefully" for *Miniature Quilts*, recommends using a tan commercial dye available for "antiquing" fabric to give brilliant whites the desired dingy look. Or you can

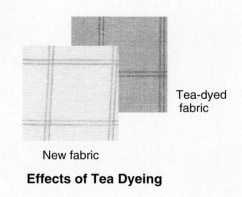

Tea-dyed fabric

New fabric

Effects of Tea Dyeing

tea dye your fabrics. To do this, use 100 percent cotton fabric, and prewash and dry it to remove the sizing. Use a small pot so the fabric bunches up and produces a time-worn, mottled look. Boil six or more tea bags in the pot; don't break the bags. Remove the pot from the stove. Dip the fabric into the pot. Don't worry about the tea bags touching the fabric, and don't stir the mixture. Let the fabric soak for 20 minutes. The resulting blotchiness will look like the authentic discoloration of time, as shown in the fabric pairs below.

Buy generic brand tea bags for tea dyeing. The cheaper brands contain more black tea, so they provide a good color. (Not to mention that they'll save you some money!)

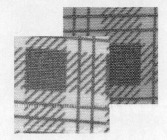

Mid-Nineteenth Century Scrap Quilts

Fabrics: Every kind of clothing fabric, especially calicoes, plaids, stripes, and large florals for borders

Colors: Madder browns, from rust to tan, mourning purples, Shaker grays, indigos, acid green, double pinks, tan (Green faded to tan and is frequently seen in antique quilts from this period.)

Quilting: Outline of the pattern; could be close or not

Blocks: Any block; usually pieced. Overall, repeating pieced patterns such as the Log Cabin were preferred.

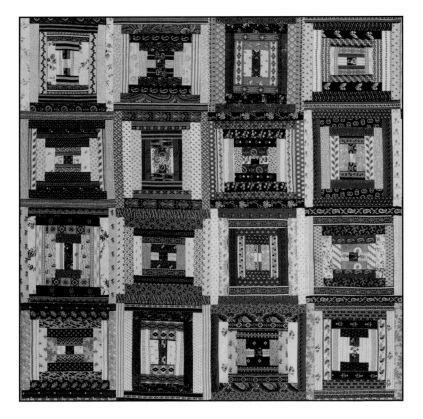

Courthouse Steps, a version of the Log Cabin pattern, is typical of mid-nineteenth century scrap quilts. In color, it contains many madder fabrics, as well as several acid greens and mourning purples. Notice the variety of prints in scale and type, including calicoes, florals, and a wonderful selection of stripes.

Late Nineteenth Century Red-and-White or Blue-and-White Quilts

Fabrics: Usually solids

Colors: Only one color, usually pure red or blue

Background: Bright white

Quilting: Any kind; could be close or not

Blocks: Any block; often repeating pieced patterns such as the Schoolhouse; sometimes alternated with white connecting blocks

*This **Red-and-White Wedding Ring** quilt, owned by Cindy Rennels, is typical of quilts made in the late nineteenth century in color and design. The fabric is a solid Turkey red, the background is a bleached white, and the quilting motifs and multiple borders are simple in design.*

Turn-of-the-Century Scrap Quilts

Fabrics: Shirtings in checks, stripes and plaids, calicoes, and conversational prints

Colors: Being scrap quilts, they contained many colors. But because of the prevailing fabric colors available at that time, these quilts had a blue, red, and white flavor and tended to contain a lot of indigo blue, double pinks, black on white prints, black on red prints, and grays.

Quilting: Usually a simple outline of the pattern; could be close or not

Blocks: Any block; often simple, overall, or repeating pieced patterns, such as the Nine Patch block

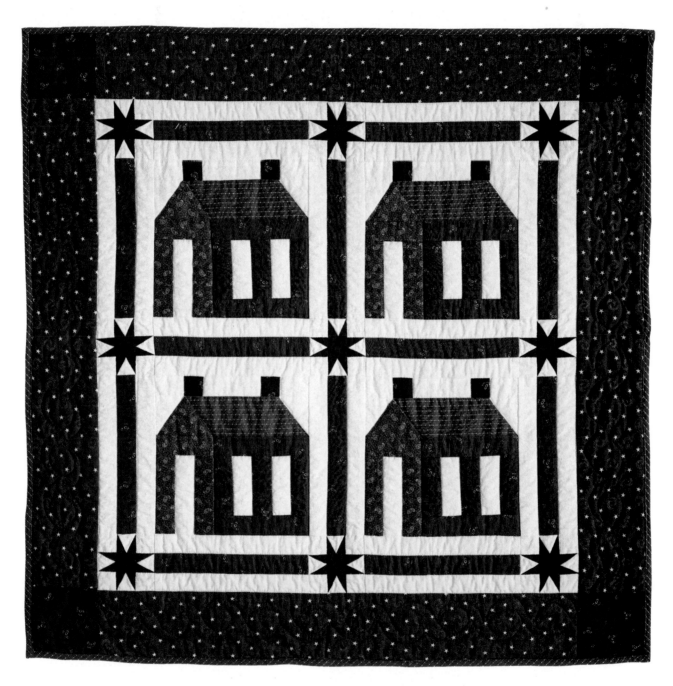

All American Schoolhouses, made by Sharyn Craig, while not an antique quilt, captures the color and flavor of turn-of-the-century quilts, which were often mainly blue, red, and white. It uses several reproduction indigo blue prints, including a celestial print typical of the time. The red calicoes are authentic in feeling, and the quilt has a slightly faded look typical of the well-used, frequently washed utilitarian quilts of that era.

1920s Pastel Quilts

Fabrics: Usually solids

Colors: One or many pastels

Background: Usually bright white and prominent

Quilting: Varied; could be close, such as small grid quilting, or not

Blocks: Many were florals, either appliquéd or pieced; baskets were a popular motif, as is evident in these two examples

*This **Carolina Lily Medallion** quilt, owned by Cindy Rennels, exemplifies 1920s quilts in color and theme. The pieced baskets float on a large, open, white space covered with grid quilting. The fabrics are all solids, and the goldish beige baskets were probably originally a soft green. Note, too, that the flower stems and sepals are a very light bluish green, a slightly faded version of depression green.*

*Many pieced quilts of the 1920s were one-color-on-white, as is this **Fruit Baskets** quilt, but pastels re-placed the strong red-on-white and blue-on-white of earlier decades. The quilting is elaborate, probably to add interest to the quiet charm of the otherwise simple quilt. Quilt owned by Cindy Rennels.*

1920s Lancaster County Amish Quilts

Fabrics: All solids, sometimes wool or sateen

Colors: Purples, blues, turquoises, magentas, dark greens, and red

Background: Usually black, although other dark colors such as green, purple, or red were also used for backgrounds. This contemporary version has a dark navy background.

Quilting: Black thread; elaborate and decorative, including feathered wreaths and borders

Blocks: Pieced; simple, large, full-quilt designs, such as Center Diamond and Bars

*This contemporary **Spiderwebs and Dewdrops** wallhanging, made by Susan Stein, is Lancaster County Amish in flavor and color, though not in design. The dark background makes the cool, pure colors appear vibrant and strong. The quilting in variegated metallic thread, while not authentic, stands out against the navy and adds sparkling accent to the open space.*

1930s Depression Quilts

Fabrics and Colors: Feedsack florals in bright and pastel colors, depression green and bright pink; greens and pinks were most often solids

Background: Unbleached muslin

Quilting: Varied from utilitarian to elaborate

Blocks: Varied; often patterns which use small scraps, such as the Wedding Ring

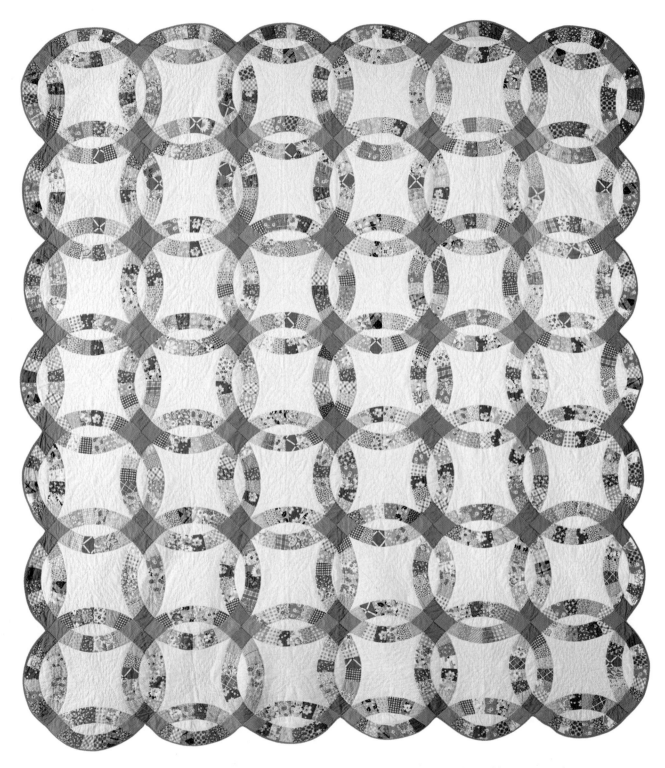

The Double Wedding Ring was a popular design in the 1930s. This **Feed Sack Wedding Ring** *quilt, owned by Bertha Rush, exhibits all of the characteristics of depression-era quilts: scraps of feedsack prints, muslin background, depression green and rosy pink solids, and lovely fill quilting.*

PLANNING EFFECTIVE

QUILT COLOR SCHEMES

Planning Effective Quilt Color Schemes

The planning stage of quiltmaking is often the most fun. It is at this stage that we consider the quilt's purpose, its future owners and their preferences, the wealth of tempting fabrics available, the myriad of quilt blocks possible, the layout, the size, the set, the quilting pattern, and so much more. It is the stage of excitement. Cutting, sewing, and quilting are more methodical, but they all lead toward the magical moment when the quilt is complete. The planning is full of challenges (and some might even say it's fraught with danger!), and color is one of the factors that makes it so.

Color will play an important role in how the finished quilt looks, so let's consider how you can use your new knowledge of color and fabric at the planning stage to help make the whole process exciting, fun, and rewarding.

LEARNING WHERE TO BEGIN

There are lots of things to consider when planning a quilt color scheme; perhaps that's why so many quilters feel overwhelmed when it comes to selecting fabrics. In this section, I've broken these color considerations down into useful bits of key information so planning your next quilt will be easy.

CONSIDER HOW COLOR AFFECTS MOOD

One of the most exciting things about color is that it affects us physically and emotionally. A great deal of research has been done on how color affects people. Although we are often unaware of it, we are affected every day by the colors that surround us. Our natural outdoor environment consists of cool sky blues and grass greens, which are soothing to us. Advertisers and product packagers use their knowledge of color-mood research to catch our attention and entice us to buy their products. They know that warm colors attract our attention, so they use them in their product packages. Hospitals and restaurants also use color to create appropriate atmospheres.

It only makes sense that as quilters we can use the same knowledge of how color affects mood to create the kinds of quilts we want. To see how to use this information effectively, here's a summary of the effects colors have on human beings.

How Colors Affect Us

Cool colors soothe and relax: Blue is placid and passive, but it can also be cold. Green is stable and tranquil, conveying hope and peacefulness.

Warm colors stimulate and excite: Red is exciting, stimulating, and agitating. It also conveys passion. Yellow is bright, cheerful, and buoyant.

Pastel colors suggest light: They are graceful and have a feeling of airiness.

Pure colors suggest buoyancy: Pure, primary colors project lightheartedness.

Muted colors suggest stability: Grayed tones are more serious than pure ones.

You often know what feeling or mood you want a quilt to convey. Now that you know how colors affect mood, you can plan a quilt that will fulfill its purpose. For example, if you want to make a quilt to comfort an ill friend, consider the peacefulness of cool colors. If it is a quilt to make a child happy, you may want to include bright, pure colors. If your quilt is to be a dramatic eye catcher at a quilt show, consider a warm color scheme.

Look at the quilt diagrams below and at the top of page 84. Each diagram is of the same quilt pattern, but the colors have been changed. See for yourself how tranquil the **Cool Colors** quilt seems when compared to the exuberance of the **Primary Colors** quilt. Note, too, that the quilt designed primarily with **Warm Colors** (see page 84) makes a powerful statement.

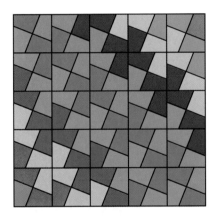

Cool Colors

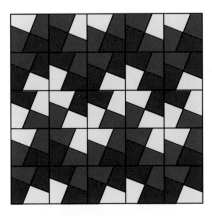

Primary Colors

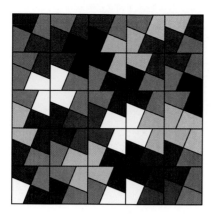

Warm Colors

CONSIDER COLOR AND CONTRAST

Using colors to set the mood is only the first step in quilt design, and quite often it is a subconscious decision. You can also add what you know about color and value contrast to your quilt planning. Since low contrast is relatively quiet while high contrast is stimulating, you can use the type of contrast that best suits your quilt. Using the same quilt diagram as in the above examples, you can see how different degrees of contrast can dramatically change the mood of an entire quilt. In the diagram below, we've used complementary contrast (red and green) and value contrast (pure red and a light, grayed green), and set them both on a pure white background. This is just one example of how different types of contrast can be used. Refer to the chapter "Color Contrast" to remind yourself of the choices.

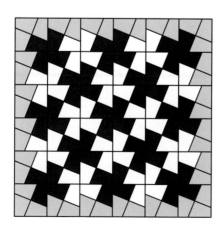

Complementary Contrast

CONSIDER THE AMOUNT OF COLOR

How much of a particular color you include will affect the relative strength of that color in the quilt. A lot of any color will make it strong in the sense that it is quite visible, even though it may not jump out at the person viewing the quilt. A quilt with a light blue background decorated with red dots will remain blue in feeling, even though the red dots will tend to jump out because they are pure and warm. Because the red dots are tiny, they will simply act as accents on the blue quilt, as shown below.

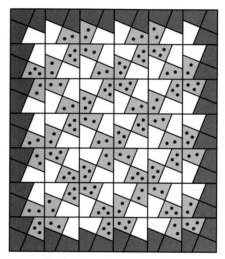

Red dots advance, yet
quilt appears blue overall

ASK YOURSELF QUESTIONS

First, ask yourself what you want the quilt to do and what mood you want it to convey. All of your color decisions depend upon the answers to these questions. What colors you choose and what kind of contrast you decide upon depend upon your quiltmaking goal.

For example, if you decide to make a quiet quilt, combine a palette of cool colors with low contrast of some kind. If you want to make a stimulating quilt, choose primarily warm colors or a mixture of warm and cool colors, and make sure your fabric selection provides high contrast of some kind.

Putting Color to the Test

Test Color Schemes

"Try before you buy" is a good motto for quilters who are unsure of their color ideas. A quick way to see how color affects a quilt design is to use crayons, markers, or colored pencils to color the design before you spend money on fabric. To do this, choose a design from a book or magazine and draw it on graph paper. Then make multiple copies on a copy machine, and color the design in different ways. Or, make one copy of the design and lay a piece of tracing paper over it. Color on the tracing paper; lift the paper and color another combination on a new sheet. You can get a lot of mileage out of only one drawing and you don't need access to a copy machine.

When you're coloring, you don't have to be precise; just a few blocks will give you an idea of how your color plan will effect the look of the quilt.

Use colored pencils rather than markers to map out your color scheme. You can use them for subtle shading to give the effect of pastel fabrics, whereas markers may be a little too bright to really represent your fabrics.

Plan a Small Quilt

Let's take a simple quilt block, the Basket block, and pretend you want to make a small quilt with just four Basket blocks with a strip-pieced sashing between them. The inspiration for this block is **Scrap Baskets with Nine-Patch Sashing,** shown at right. This scrap quilt uses many fabrics on an off-white background. Notice that some baskets stand out because of contrast of value, while others get lost for the same reason.

In this color exercise, you'll be trying several different color variations of the same pattern. It's the color decisions that will affect how the quilt will look. Even with this simple design, you still need to ask yourself some questions:

• Do you want your quilt to be a bright or a tranquil one?
• Do you want the baskets to stand out against the background or blend in with it?
• Which do you want to stand out more, the baskets or the sashing?

Here are several color options to consider after you have answered these questions. Suppose I want a quiet quilt in which the baskets stand out against the background and are stronger than the sashing, as shown in **Color Option 1** on page 86. I can choose several cool blues and greens for a quiet effect, but I need high contrast so the baskets will stand out against the white background. I can't achieve high contrast through color because the blues and greens are closely related, so I need to achieve it through contrast of value. To do that, I can make my background very light and my baskets either dark or pure.

Scrap Baskets with Nine-Patch Sashing
made by Wilma Sestric

If the color combination seems too dull, I can add a little of a warm color, such as a pale tint of yellow. If I put the yellow in the baskets and keep the sashing cool, the warm will help emphasize the baskets.

Take a look at the resulting basket quilt I've planned. Notice how the blue, green, and yellow in medium to dark values on a white background work together to make a calm color scheme without being too quiet or boring.

Color Option 2 shows what happens when I answer the same set of questions differently because I'd like a vibrant quilt. I choose the complementary colors red and green because complements always provide high color contrast, and add a neutral white background. Remembering that it's important to use complements in unequal amounts, I opt to use more red than green. The resulting quilt is high in value contrast as well as color contrast. Not only do the blocks provide contrast, but the bold sashing does, too. If I want to de-emphasize the sashing, I can make it predominantly green.

Take a look at the Basket quilt in **Color Option 3**, shown below at right. My answers to the basic color questions are less clear in this quilt. The cool greens and blues in the baskets at first suggest a peaceful color scheme, especially when combined with the quilters' neutrals. But for fun, I want to create a strong sashing, so I choose red. The baskets still stand out against the background because of value contrast and because the background is a neutral beige, yet the bright red sashing makes a strong secondary design in the quilt top.

Now try your hand at using color to change a quilt using the **Scrap Basket Color Plan** on the opposite page. Make a few copies of the color plan, either with a photocopier or by tracing. Play freely with colored pencils to make a color scheme. Then try another color scheme after asking yourself the three questions at the top of page 85. Pretend you want a certain effect and see if you can achieve it. In just minutes you'll be able to play with different colors and see the variety of looks that are possible.

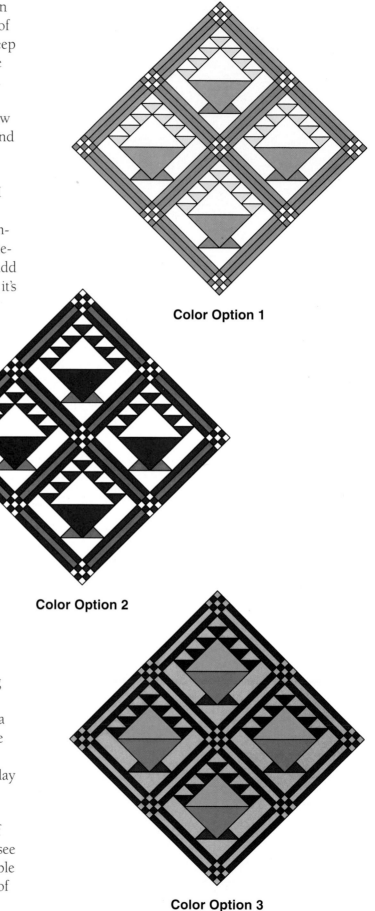

Color Option 1

Color Option 2

Color Option 3

Make your own Basket quilt color scheme

Scrap Basket Color Plan

USE COLOR TO EMPHASIZE PARTS OF A DESIGN

The Basket block is a simple design. Although we could emphasize the basket or the sashing depending on where we put certain colors, the design remains the same. Many blocks, however, can look completely different depending upon how you color them. One such example is the **Snowball and Nine Patch** combination, shown below.

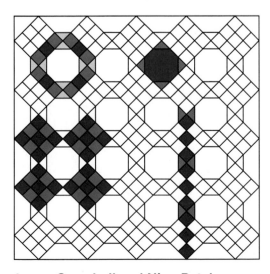

Snowball and Nine Patch

Setting these two quilt blocks together in a quilt top is fairly common. Yet you can create a variety of different effects with this simple design just by varying the color placement. The partially colored diagram below at left shows that when different parts of a design are emphasized, the resulting quilts will be completely different! Here, too, coloring with pencils is a quick way to explore the possibilities of a block.

Emphasize a Background—or Not

Coloring is a good way to try out different background colors, too. The **Double Wedding Ring Color Plan**, shown below, illustrates how different the same quilt would look if you changed just one fabric—the background. You don't even have to color the entire drawing. Just color enough to get the feeling of the backgrounds you are considering.

Double Wedding Ring Color Plan

Practice Makes Perfect

Since it's a lot easier (and much less expensive) to plan a quilt on paper than out of fabric, we've provided three sets of quilt blocks that you can use for your own creative exercises. Look at the original quilts from which we've taken the blocks (notice they are all variations of a simple Nine Patch block), study the sample colorings we have provided, and then try your hand at designing your own quilts. Try to emphasize different areas of the overall design with each color plan.

Now's a great time to experiment with a color scheme that you've never worked with before. There's no fabric investment to make, and you might even surprise yourself and enjoy the result! After all, this is always a fun part of quiltmaking.

Summer's End
made by Judy Miller

Color ideas for Summer's End

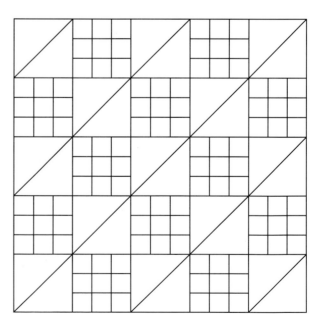

Create your own color scheme

Oklahoma Nine Patch
made by Carolyn Miller

Summer's End, shown on the opposite page, features a strong diagonal line. Notice how the line of the quilt design can be emphasized or de-emphasized, however, simply by changing the contrast of value used in the triangle squares that separate the Nine Patch blocks.

Oklahoma Nine Patch, shown at left, also incorporates diagonal lines in the quilt design, but this time the diagonals are set in a barn-raising style. By changing the original black and white triangle squares to a more placid, analogous color scheme, the quilt will take on a whole new look. Yet another approach would be to use an Amish color scheme for a third entirely different look.

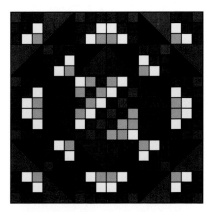

Color ideas for Oklahoma Nine Patch

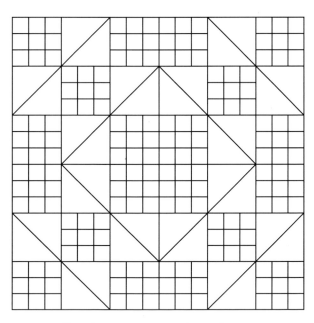

Create your own color scheme

On the Road Again…Paducah Bound, is also a Nine Patch quilt, but in this quilt design, the blocks were turned on point to achieve the diagonal, medallion-type setting. Notice that by altering the color choices you can emphasize different areas of the design so either diamonds, nine patches, or pinwheels become more visible. What area of the design would you emphasize with color?

On the Road Again…Paducah Bound
made by Nancy Chizek

Color ideas for Paducah Bound

Create your own color scheme

Planning Effective Quilt Color Schemes

TIPS ON CHOOSING COLORS

A TRIED-AND-TRUE COLOR PLAN

One of the easiest ways to choose a beautiful color scheme for a quilt is to use a theme fabric. A theme fabric is one that contains several colors and is often a large, busy print. Because the fabric designer knew all about color and chose harmonious colors, you are guaranteed a successful color scheme if you use this fabric as the basis for your color selections.

The first step is to find a fabric you like that contains several colors. Carry the fabric around as you search for additional fabrics in these colors. Look at the sample fabrics below. Notice that the theme fabric contains analogous warm colors, a neutral, and contrast of value. If you pull out the colors as you look for coordinating fabrics—such as beige, lavender, maroon, or rusty red—your color scheme is set!

In addition to following the colors in a theme fabric, pay attention to how much each color is used in the theme fabric. If it's used just a little, that's a good indication that you should use just a little of that color in your quilt, too.

The theme fabric system of color planning works at any time and is particularly useful for beginning quilters who may be unsure of their own color preferences.

STRIKE A BALANCE

You already know that when working with complementary colors, it's important to use more of one complement than of the other. The same sense of proportion holds true when you work with advancing and receding colors in a quilt. For the best results, use more of the receding colors (cool, light, or muted colors) than you do of the advancing colors (warm, pure, or dark colors). If you use too many strong, advancing colors, they will overpower the quilt.

The two Schoolhouse blocks shown below illustrate this point. Imagine how overpowering a whole quilt made from the red and yellow blocks with that busy sashing would look. There are so many components made of advancing, strong colors that the viewer wouldn't know where to look first. In the second block, the red house stands out nicely against the aqua sky, and the dark blue sashing and red stars make a nice frame around the house without detracting from it.

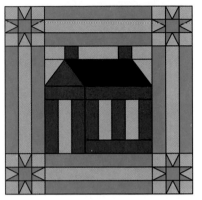

Too many advancing colors; house, sashing, stars, and background all fight for attention

Using more receding colors lets house stand out, yet sashing and stars frame it nicely

A LITTLE YELLOW GOES A LONG WAY

As we discussed in the chapter "The Color Wheel," yellow is the strongest and most brilliant color on the color wheel. You need much less yellow in proportion to other colors.

Look at the **Mennonite Four Patch/ Nine Patch** quilt at right. The color scheme is simple: brown, green, red, and yellow. The quiet, earthy brown is used in the greatest proportion and the yellow, red, and green are used in about the same small proportions. Notice how you see the yellow grid pattern immediately and then the red patches. The yellow takes over this quilt, just as it always does. Can you imagine how this quilt would have looked if the quiltmaker had swapped the placement of the vibrant yellow and the soft brown? Don't be afraid to use yellow in your quilts, just use it sparingly, or soften its power by using a pale tint of yellow.

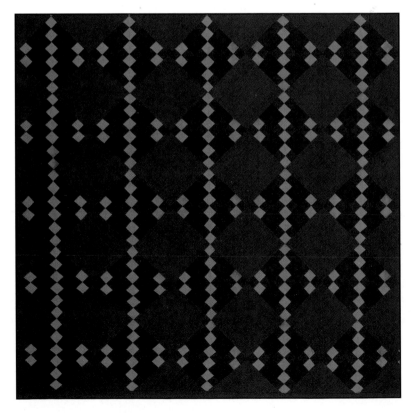

Mennonite Four Patch/Nine Patch
owned by Joan Townsend

Never Use a Color Only Once

Be sure to use every color in your quilt more than once. Echo the colors in some way, whether in small pieces or in large elements somewhere else. Repeating colors will help to balance the quilt. For example, take a look at **Simply Charming,** below. Notice how the bright yellow-green diamonds seem to pop off the page. If this shade of green had been used in only one spot, your eye would have been drawn to that area of

the quilt, where it would have stopped. Instead, the quiltmaker used this vivid green in several places so it became a tool to move your eye over the entire quilt top. Repeated use of this green makes it seem less unexpected.

Using a color more than once doesn't mean you have to use the same exact fabric more than once. The quilt below is a charm quilt, with each patch cut from a different fabric. The fabrics aren't repeated, but the colors are.

Simply Charming
made by Edith Zimmer

CHOOSING THE RIGHT BORDER

The right border can make or break a great quilt. Here are four important tips to help you select the right fabric and make sure your quilt gets the border it deserves.

1. Watch your proportions. The amount of border fabric is usually huge in comparison to the patchwork pieces or appliqué in the center of the quilt. Therefore, whatever color you put in the border will make a very strong statement. If you don't want too bold a border, select a soothing color fabric.

2. Echo colors in the quilt top. The border is a good place to echo a color you want to emphasize from the center design. If you choose the strongest color, however, remember that you will be using a lot of it and it may be too dominant and overpower your quilt.

Conversely, if you choose too light a color, the border will appear to fall off the quilt. It will be lifeless or dull and might as well not even be there. Consider the second strongest or a moderately strong color from the center for an appropriate border color.

3. Don't start a new color in the border. A border needs to blend with the quilt somehow. If you are using a new fabric, which quilters often do, be sure it repeats a color or a value found in the center of the quilt. The border fabric should also be of the same intensity and mood as the center. It's fine to use a new fabric, just not a whole new color.

4. Use a narrow inner border of a stronger color. If you want to repeat a strong color but don't want to use too much of it, use it in a narrow inner border. Then finish off the quilt with a second, wider border made of a less powerful color. This was done successfully in the **Sunshine and Shadow** quilt, shown below. The quiltmaker brought out the red in the Log Cabin blocks nicely by repeating it in the narrow inner border. Had the red been used in the wide outer border, it would have overpowered the dramatic pattern of the quilt. Used sparingly, however, it makes a strong echo to the many red prints in the Log Cabin blocks. The outer border repeats the value and color of many of the center fabrics, and its neutral brown color frames the quilt but doesn't detract from the design.

Sunshine and Shadow
made by Bettina Havig and owned by Joyce Gross

BINDING:
YOUR FINAL COLOR CHOICE

The binding is your last chance to make or break your color scheme, and it's also a good place to echo a strong color. Because it is so narrow, it provides just a touch of the color you choose. A bit of color contrast is also fun, and it shows off the binding nicely.

Barn Raising, shown below, illustrates all of the key points on selecting borders and bindings. The electric blue inner border repeats and brings out a color that was used sparingly within the quilt. It would probably have been too strong a color for the wide outer border, so a calmer dark blue is used there. It, too, repeats a color from the center. The fuschia binding, however, begins something new at the very outside of the quilt. Although it is purer and thus stronger than the related colors used in the center, it is an analogous color to the others in the quilt, which helps it blend in. However, the fuschia is still distinct enough to add that final bit of whimsy and fun.

Barn Raising
made by Mark Stratton, quilted by an Amish family

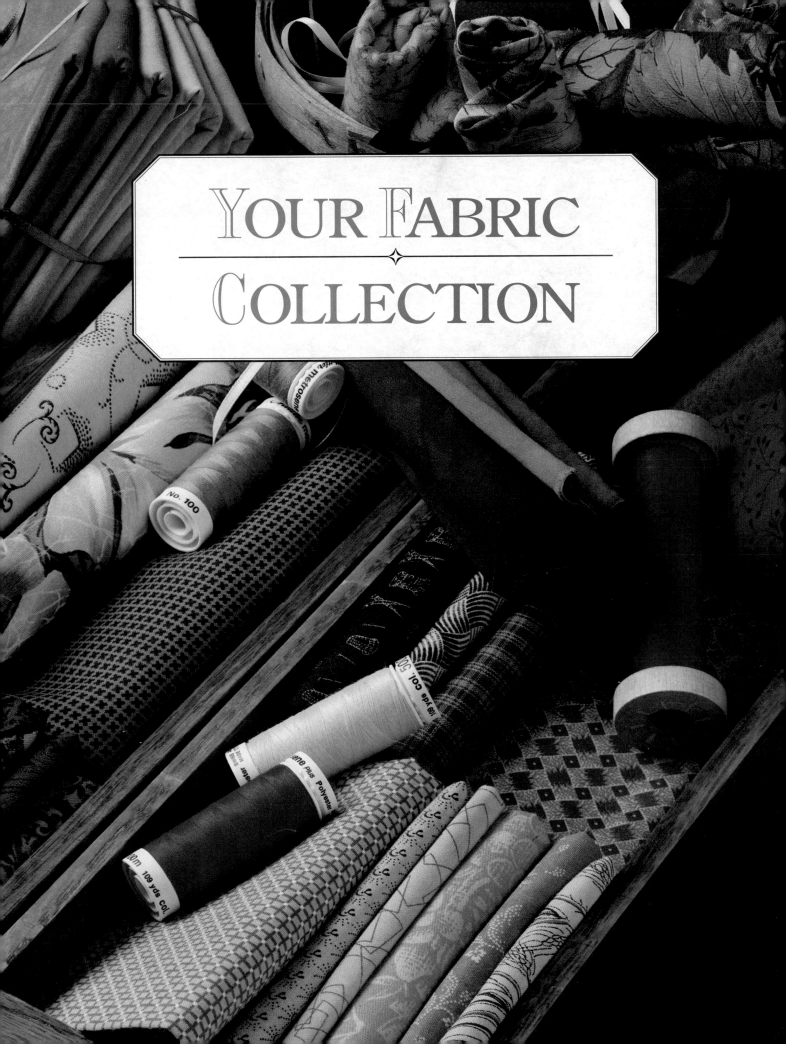

YOUR FABRIC
COLLECTION

YOUR FABRIC COLLECTION

As soon as you set aside the leftover fabrics from your first quilt, you've begun a fabric collection! For quilters, fabric is our resource. We may add to that resource frugally by simply saving the scraps from each quilt we make, or we may begin to collect ahead as we see fabric we love and feel sure we will need at some time in the future.

This chapter covers three concepts that will help you plan your quilts and build your fabric collection. First, we'll analyze quilt patterns so you can make a fabric checklist for any quilt you want to make—in any color scheme. Then we'll look at your personal fabric stash to see what you have, what you don't have, and what you can do to systematically add to your collection and expand its versatility. Finally, you'll find ideas for organizing and storing your precious yards, fat quarters, and leftover bits of fabric so they'll be protected and ready to use when you need them.

ANALYZING QUILTS FOR COLOR

Use the **Color Inspiration** chart below to help you analyze the quilts in this book and others that you see and like. It will help you determine why you like a particular quilt and what aspects of its color, contrast, and design you'd like to incorporate into a quilt of your own. Then you'll be better prepared to plan and design your own color schemes.

If the idea of analyzing quilts in this systematic way seems a little foreign or unnatural to you, don't worry. After you try it a few times the process will become easy and almost automatic when you view a quilt, whether you admire it in a book or see it hanging at a quilt show.

Make a quilt photo album to hold snapshots you take at quilt shows or classes you attend. Slip a photocopy of this chart in next to the quilts you particularly like, and use it to jot down notes or ideas about colors and fabrics for future reference.

Color Inspiration

QUILT NAME: _____

What color hits me first? Why? _____

List the colors used: _____

_____

_____

Check for the types of contrast.

Are they present? How are they used?

☐ *Contrast of Value* _____

☐ *Complementary Contrast* _____

☐ *Warm-Cool Contrast* _____

☐ *Pure Color Contrast* _____

☐ *Contrast of Intensity* _____

High contrast or low contrast? _____

What color is the background? _____

Are neutrals used? Which ones? _____

Determine the mood of the quilt.

Choose one or more adjectives to describe how this quilt makes you feel: _____

What created that mood? _____

_____

Why does this quilt appeal to me? _____

_____

PLANNING MY NEXT QUILT

Record information about your quilt in the **Quilt Planner** below, and fill in the information and fabric swatches on the opposite page. Copy the pages so you can use them again, each time including a picture or sketch of the quilt design for color planning purposes. You can paste up fabric swatches you're considering, then take the quilt planner and samples along when you shop for additional fabrics.

Quilt Planner

QUILT PATTERN: _____

QUILT SIZE: _____

Number of main design blocks needed: _____   Borders: _____

Number of alternate blocks needed: _____   Binding: _____

Insert Quilt Drawing or Color Plan here:

KEY QUESTIONS TO HELP MY PLANNING

There are many factors to consider when planning a quilt. Before you choose a block and begin picking out fabric, ask yourself the following questions:

What mood do I want the quilt to convey?

_____
_____
_____
_____

What colors will help me convey this mood?

_____
_____
_____
_____

What kind of contrast will help me convey this mood?

_____
_____
_____
_____

What part of the design do I want to emphasize?

_____
_____
_____
_____

What neutral or neutrals will I use?

_____
_____
_____
_____

How many fabrics do I need?

_____
_____
_____
_____

FABRICS SWATCHES AND YARDAGE REQUIREMENTS

Organize your fabrics in order by how much they will be used in the quilt, and jot down yardage requirements for an easy-reference shopping list.

Prior to shopping, color or paste fabrics in the blocks to remind yourself of the color fabrics you'll be looking for.

Fabrics	Yardage Needed
Fabric A	_____
Fabric B	_____
Fabric C	_____
Fabric D	_____
Fabric E	_____

Color or Paste Swatches

Developing a Versatile Fabric Collection

When it comes to planning or selecting the fabrics for a quilt, there are two ways to go about it. You can either take your quilt book or pattern to the fabric store with you and purchase all new fabrics for the quilt you want to make, or you can "shop" at home first. Once your fabric collection begins to grow, you'll have the option of looking through your many fabrics and selecting ones you'd like to use for a project. You can mix and match, add and delete, spread the fabrics out over the table or floor, and really begin working with the fabrics as a planning tool. Then you'll only need to shop for fabrics to fill in the gaps, rather than purchasing enough fabric for an entire quilt.

Analyzing Your Fabrics

To make your fabric collection really work for you, however, it is important to know what colors and print styles you have readily available to you and which types you'll need to purchase. Rather than rummaging through an insurmountable stack of unorganized fabrics (or through boxes or storage bins), it's really helpful if you can get a good idea of your collection's strengths and weaknesses at a glance.

Later in this section you'll find handy ideas for organizing your growing collection. Here, however, we'll focus on the kinds of fabrics you've been collecting and what gaps might be developing. For instance, do you tend to have a lot of variety in red prints, but seem to be lacking purple ones? Or do you seem to favor grayed or toned-down colors over pure, intense ones?

We each have our favorite colors and styles of prints, whether they be large scale, pastel florals, or brightly colored homespun plaids. But remember, it's the variety of fabrics you use that will spice up your quilts, so it's good to have all styles of prints and an excellent variety of color available to work with in your sewing room. On the next 12 pages you'll find a **Color and Print Analysis** chart for each of the 12 colors in the basic color wheel. These charts show examples of the pure colors and light, dark, and grayed values of each color. Next to each color value there is space to record how many different fabrics you own of each color and print style. By evaluating your entire group of fabrics and determining how many pieces you have of each color, you'll quickly see where your collection is strong and where it could use some additional fabrics to round out the color wheel.

Yellow	Color and Print Analysis				
	Floral	Geometric	Abstract	Ethnic	Solid
Pure — Small scale					
Pure — Medium scale					
Pure — Large scale					
Light — Small scale					
Light — Medium scale					
Light — Large scale					
Dark — Small scale					
Dark — Medium scale					
Dark — Large scale					
Grayed — Small scale					
Grayed — Medium scale					
Grayed — Large scale					

Yellow-orange

Color and Print Analysis

		Floral	Geometric	Abstract	Ethnic	Solid
Pure	Small scale					
	Medium scale					
	Large scale					
Light	Small scale					
	Medium scale					
	Large scale					
Dark	Small scale					
	Medium scale					
	Large scale					
Grayed	Small scale					
	Medium scale					
	Large scale					

$\mathcal{O}$range

		Floral	Geometric	Abstract	Ethnic	Solid
Pure	Small scale					
	Medium scale					
	Large scale					
Light	Small scale					
	Medium scale					
	Large scale					
Dark	Small scale					
	Medium scale					
	Large scale					
Grayed	Small scale					
	Medium scale					
	Large scale					

Red-orange

		Floral	Geometric	Abstract	Ethnic	Solid
Pure	Small scale					
	Medium scale					
	Large scale					
Light	Small scale					
	Medium scale					
	Large scale					
Dark	Small scale					
	Medium scale					
	Large scale					
Grayed	Small scale					
	Medium scale					
	Large scale					

$\mathcal{R}ed$	Color and Print Analysis				
	Floral	**Geometric**	**Abstract**	**Ethnic**	**Solid**

Pure

	Floral	Geometric	Abstract	Ethnic	Solid
Small scale					
Medium scale					
Large scale					

Light

	Floral	Geometric	Abstract	Ethnic	Solid
Small scale					
Medium scale					
Large scale					

Dark

	Floral	Geometric	Abstract	Ethnic	Solid
Small scale					
Medium scale					
Large scale					

Grayed

	Floral	Geometric	Abstract	Ethnic	Solid
Small scale					
Medium scale					
Large scale					

$\mathcal{R}ed$-$violet$		Color and Print Analysis				
		Floral	Geometric	Abstract	Ethnic	Solid
Pure	Small scale					
	Medium scale					
	Large scale					
Light	Small scale					
	Medium scale					
	Large scale					
Dark	Small scale					
	Medium scale					
	Large scale					
Grayed	Small scale					
	Medium scale					
	Large scale					

V*iolet*

Color and Print Analysis

		Floral	Geometric	Abstract	Ethnic	Solid
Pure	Small scale					
	Medium scale					
	Large scale					
Light	Small scale					
	Medium scale					
	Large scale					
Dark	Small scale					
	Medium scale					
	Large scale					
Grayed	Small scale					
	Medium scale					
	Large scale					

Blue-violet	Color and Print Analysis				
	Floral	Geometric	Abstract	Ethnic	Solid
Pure — Small scale					
Medium scale					
Large scale					
Light — Small scale					
Medium scale					
Large scale					
Dark — Small scale					
Medium scale					
Large scale					
Grayed — Small scale					
Medium scale					
Large scale					

***B**lue*	Color and Print Analysis				
	Floral	**Geometric**	**Abstract**	**Ethnic**	**Solid**
Pure — Small scale					
Pure — Medium scale					
Pure — Large scale					
Light — Small scale					
Light — Medium scale					
Light — Large scale					
Dark — Small scale					
Dark — Medium scale					
Dark — Large scale					
Grayed — Small scale					
Grayed — Medium scale					
Grayed — Large scale					

Blue-green	Color and Print Analysis				
	Floral	Geometric	Abstract	Ethnic	Solid
Pure — Small scale					
Pure — Medium scale					
Pure — Large scale					
Light — Small scale					
Light — Medium scale					
Light — Large scale					
Dark — Small scale					
Dark — Medium scale					
Dark — Large scale					
Grayed — Small scale					
Grayed — Medium scale					
Grayed — Large scale					

$\mathcal{G}$*reen*	Color and Print Analysis				
	Floral	**Geometric**	**Abstract**	**Ethnic**	**Solid**
Pure — Small scale					
Pure — Medium scale					
Pure — Large scale					
Light — Small scale					
Light — Medium scale					
Light — Large scale					
Dark — Small scale					
Dark — Medium scale					
Dark — Large scale					
Grayed — Small scale					
Grayed — Medium scale					
Grayed — Large scale					

$\mathcal{Y}$ellow-green

		Color and Print Analysis				
		Floral	**Geometric**	**Abstract**	**Ethnic**	**Solid**
Pure	Small scale					
	Medium scale					
	Large scale					
Light	Small scale					
	Medium scale					
	Large scale					
Dark	Small scale					
	Medium scale					
	Large scale					
Grayed	Small scale					
	Medium scale					
	Large scale					

FABRIC SHOPPING LIST

Once you've determined the state of your fabric collection, you can plan for future growth. If you've found that you need more yellows or greens or grays, you can set out to remedy the situation. The **Fabric Wish List,** shown below, is a handy checklist that you can take with you each time you visit your local quilt shop or fabric store, when you travel to quilt shows, or as you browse through mail-order catalogs.

Of course, you don't have to dramatically increase the number of fabrics you own right away. Filling in the shopping list can just serve as a reminder of the types of fabrics you want to look for when you have the opportunity. Try purchasing one or two of the colors from your checklist the next time you're shopping. You'll be surprised how easy it is to acquire a wonderful array of fabrics in a relatively short period of time. Soon, you won't have to make a special trip to the fabric store to begin a new quilt. Everything you need will be available right in the convenience—and comfort—of your own sewing room.

 *A painless way to grow your fabric collection is to always buy a little too much for each project. An extra ⅛ or ¼ yard of each fabric will add a lot more variety to your collection— and your future quilts—without costing a bundle.*

Fabric Wish List

Check each box that applies for the colors you need. For example, if you need yellow fabrics, make a check to indicate whether you need to buy pure or light yellow. Then indicate the print scale and style of prints you'd like by using the codes below. Photocopy this blank Wish List so you can reuse it as often as you like.

Key:

Print Scale	Print Style	
S = small	F = floral	E = ethnic
M = medium	G = geometric	S = solid
L = large	A = abstract	

	Dark	Medium	Light	Grayed	Pure	Print Scale	Print Style
Yellow							
Yellow-orange							
Orange							
Red-orange							
Red							
Red-violet							
Violet							
Blue-violet							
Blue							
Blue-green							
Green							
Yellow-green							
Black							
Gray							
White							
Quilters' neutrals (beiges to browns)							

What to Do with All That Fabric

Prepare Before Storing

Wash and dry fabric as soon as you bring it into your home. Washing helps get rid of excess dye, removes the sizing, and pre-shrinks the fabric. Fabric may not need ironing if you remove it from the dryer immediately, but do iron it if it is wrinkled. Then fold it to the size that fits your storage area and put it away. If you put away fabric that has some wrinkles that haven't been pressed, it will be much harder, maybe even impossible, to get them out later without rewashing the fabric.

Some fabrics bleed more than others because they contain more dye or because their dye is less stable. To save time and conserve water, you can prewash a variety of fabrics together in one washer load or basin. To keep colors from running and ruining other fabrics while pre-washing, add a dye fixative (such as Synthropol) to the water. This product is used by hand-dyers to set the color in fabrics.

Organize Your Storage Space

At some point in your quilting life, storing fabric will probably become a challenge. Storage cabinets and shelves are available in many sizes and price ranges. Stores that specialize in storage and closet design have excellent units that we quilters can adapt to our needs. Whatever type of storage or display area you have or plan, keep in mind that fabric needs to be protected from excessive light (natural and indoor), dampness, and dust. Here are some easy storage ideas that just about any sewing area can accommodate:

• Stackable, plastic storage boxes. They keep fabric clean and tidy, and the see-through type lets you see what's inside so you know without opening every box whether fabrics are sorted by colors or by darks and lights.

• Under-the-bed, flat storage boxes. If your sewing room is small, you can use this type of container to stash fabric out of the way under the bed or the sofa.

• Closet shelves. Storing fabric in the closet keeps it out of the light. If your closet has only one shelf overhead, consider adding several more at lower heights for easy access. When the door is closed, your fabric is out of sight and the room is neat. This works well when your sewing room is also the guest room or the family room.

• Open shelves. This method keeps fabric close at hand where it can inspire you and be ready to jump off a shelf and into a quilt at a moment's notice. The drawback, however, is that depending on the lighting conditions in your sewing room, the fabric can be exposed to harsh sunlight.

If you like the ready-access open shelves provide but are concerned about sunlight fading your fabrics, attach a roller shade to the shelf or slip fabric with a rod pocket over a curtain rod and attach it to the top shelf of your storage area. Pull down the shade or slide the curtain across the shelves to protect your fabrics when they're not in use.

Organize Your Fabric

Once you have lots of fabric, it's time to organize it for your convenience. That way, you'll be able to find a particular fabric immediately when you need it. Here are the considerations I use in sorting my fabric. Perhaps they may fit your needs or give you some ideas for organizing your fabric collection.

Sort by Color

I generally sort my fabrics by color and put all values and intensities within a color group together. This gives me instant perspective on where my collection is limited, and I can set about filling in the gaps on future shopping expeditions.

Separate Piles

I separate out certain kinds of fabric so that I can find them easily. Here are the types of piles I like to keep, but depending upon the fabrics you collect, you may have one or two others to add.

Solids. I find it easier to keep solids separate from my prints, since I often use them in different types of projects. For example, when I'm working on an Amish-style quilt where I would use only solids, I can reach for what I need without a lot of searching. Within the set of solids, I sort by color.

Wide stripes. These often contain many colors and would be hard to classify by any one color.

Large pieces. I keep my eyes open for sale fabrics I would like to use on the backs of my quilts and buy many yards. I store these fabrics on a separate shelf so I know they are to be used for quilt backs. This keeps me from cutting off bits of fabric for various projects until I don't have enough left for a backing.

Hand-dyed fabrics. These are usually small pieces and they tend to get lost in large piles of fabric. Besides, I usually want to reserve them for special projects. I subdivide the hand-dyed stack by color.

Antique fabrics. These precious fabrics are both fragile and expensive, so I store them separately, too.

Temporary Piles

I often separate fabrics temporarily by current projects or themes, such as a stack of depression fabrics for a period quilt or a pile of plaids for a folk art quilt.

Determine the yardage to buy of a particular fabric by how you think it will be used. For example, a large-scale theme print could be used for borders or setting squares, so 3 yards or so would be a wise purchase. Accent fabrics can be as small as quarter- or fat quarter-yards and still be useful. For quilt backings, consider whether the fabric is likely to be used for a wall-hanging or a bed-size quilt. Remember, a queen- or king-size quilt can require as much as 7 to 10 yards of fabric!

START PLANNING YOUR NEXT QUILT

Now that you have gained a better understanding and appreciation of how colors and print styles work together to add a wonderful visual texture to your projects, you're armed and ready to plan and stitch your best quilt ever! Knowing how colors work and behave together will give you the confidence to try new ideas and color schemes. I hope that you have as much fun experimenting with different color and fabric options to design your own quilts as I have designing mine.

About the Author

Susan McKelvey is a well-known expert on color who is especially interested in making color understandable to quilters. She has written several books and articles on color, as well as on other quilting subjects, such as writing on quilts and designing quilt labels. Through her company, Wallflower Designs, she designs and distributes quilting books, patterns, and supplies. She teaches quilting throughout the United States, and her quilts have appeared in quilt shows, galleries, and museums.

Before discovering quiltmaking in 1977, Susan earned her B.A. in English at Cornell College and her M.A. at the University of Chicago. After earning her M.A., Susan then taught English in Illinois, Iowa, and Maryland, and with the Peace Corps in Ethiopia. She has also worked as a test development manager at Westinghouse Learning Corporation.

Susan and her husband, parents of two college-age children, currently live in rural Anne Arundel County, Maryland, with two rescued golden retrievers and two beautiful cats, all of whom think they were born to grace quilts!

Resources and Recommended Reading

I found the books listed below to be valuable resources as I researched material for Creative Ideas for Color and Fabric. I highly recommend any of these titles to you if you are interested in further study of color or fabric styles.

Albers, Joseph. *Interaction of Color.* New Haven: Yale University Press, 1975.
Birren, Faber. *Creative Color.* West Chester: Schiffer Publishing, 1987.
Brackman, Barbara. *Clues in the Calico: Identifying and Dating Quilts.* McLean, Va.: EPM Publications, 1989.
Meller, Susan, and Elffers, Joost. *Textile Designs: Two Hundred Years of European & American Patterns for Printed Fabrics.* New York: Henry N. Abrams, Publishers, 1991.
McKelvey, Susan. *Color for Quilters.* vol. II. Millersville: Wallflower Designs, 1994.
Nehring, Jane. "Aging Gracefully: Gentle Ways to Make A New Quilt Look Old." *Miniature Quilts,* Issue 17, p. 21.
Quiller, Stephen. Color Choices. New York: Watson-Guptill Publications, 1989.

ACKNOWLEDGMENTS

Companies Who Contributed Fabric

Our thanks go to the companies who generously contributed the fabrics that so beautifully illustrate the color concepts in this book:

EZ International
Fasco
Marcus Brothers
Osage County Quilt Factory
P&B Textiles
Piney Woods
RJR
The Souder Store
South Sea Imports

The Quiltmakers

We also gratefully thank the many exceptional quiltmakers and collectors who graciously permitted us to show their quilts as examples of the principles of working with color and fabric:

Martha Bastian, Mexico, Missouri
Barbara Berliner, Columbia, Missouri
Nancy Chizek, Ann Arbor, Michigan
Sharyn Craig, El Cajon, California
DSI Studios, Evansville, Indiana
Jane Graff, Delafield, Wisconsin
Joyce Gross, Petaluma, California
Doris Heitman, Williamsburg, Iowa
Becky Herdle, Rochester, New York
Naoko Anne Ito, Berkeley, California
Kathryn Jones, Marshall, Missouri
Kathryn Kuhn, Monument, Colorado
Edith Leeper, Columbia, Missouri
Shirley McElderry, Ottumwa, Iowa
Irene Metz, Harleysville, Pennsylvania
Carolyn Miller, Santa Cruz, California
Judy Miller, Columbia, Maryland

Museum of the American Quilter's Society, Paducah, Kentucky
Lucille Powell, Gilbertsville, Pennsylvania
Julee Prose, Ottumwa, Iowa
Annie Segal for Quilters' Newsletter Magazine, Golden, Colorado
Randolph County Historical Society, Moberly, Missouri
Cindy Rennels, Clinton, Oklahoma
Bertha Rush, Hatfield, Pennsylvania
Wilma Sestric, Ballwin, Missouri
Susan Stein, St. Paul, Minnesota
Karen Stone, Dallas, Texas
Carly and Mark Stratton, Pasadena, California
Joan Townsend of Oh Suzannah, Lebanon, Ohio
Elsie Vredenberg, Tustin, Michigan
Edith Zimmer, San Diego, California

INDEX

THE CLASSIC AMERICAN
QUILT COLLECTION

◇

All of the quilts shown in Creative Ideas for Color and Fabric *are featured as how-to projects in other volumes of* The Classic American Quilt Collection. *Look for these books at your local quilt shop or book store. Or, call* 1-800-763-2531 *for more information or to order any of these books. Member discounts are available.*

Amish

Baskets

Log Cabin

Nine Patch

One Patch

Quilting Made Easy

Schoolhouse

Stars

Wedding Ring